UNITED STATES DEPARTMENT OF THE INTERIOR
HAROLD L. ICKES : SECRETARY

OFFICE OF EDUCATION : WILLIAM JOHN COOPER
COMMISSIONER

SECONDARY EDUCATION FOR NEGROES

BY

AMBROSE CALIVER

BULLETIN, 1932, NO. 17

NATIONAL SURVEY OF SECONDARY EDUCATION

MONOGRAPH NO. 7

NEGRO UNIVERSITIES PRESS
NEW YORK

NOTE

Ambrose Caliver, the author of this monograph, is specialist in Negro education of the Office of Education. William John Cooper, United States Commissioner of Education, is director of the NATIONAL SURVEY OF SECONDARY EDUCA-TION; *Leonard V. Koos, professor of secondary education at the University of Chicago, is associate director; and Carl A. Jessen, specialist in secondary education of the Office of Education, is coordinator.*

[II]

Originally published in 1933
by U.S. Government Printing Office, Washington, D.C.

Reprinted 1969 by
Negro Universities Press
A DIVISION OF GREENWOOD PUBLISHING CORP.
NEW YORK

SBN 8371-2046-2

PRINTED IN UNITED STATES OF AMERICA

CONTENTS

CONTENTS

CONTENTS

LETTER OF TRANSMITTAL

DEPARTMENT OF THE INTERIOR,
OFFICE OF EDUCATION,
Washington, D. C., June, 1933.

SIR: Within a period of 30 years the high-school enrollment has increased from a little over 10 per cent of the population of high-school age to more than 50 per cent of that population. This enrollment is so unusual for a secondary school that it has attracted the attention of Europe, where only 8 to 10 per cent attend secondary schools. Many European educators have said that we are educating too many people. I believe, however, that the people of the United States are now getting a new conception of education. They are coming to look upon education as a preparation for citizenship and for daily life rather than for the money return which comes from it. They are looking upon the high school as a place for their boys and girls to profit at a period when they are not yet acceptable to industry.

In order that we may know where we stand in secondary education, the membership of the North Central Association of Colleges and Secondary Schools four years ago took the lead in urging a study. It seemed to them that it was wise for such a study to be made by the Government of the United States rather than by a private foundation, for if such an agency studied secondary education it might be accused, either rightly or wrongly, of a bias toward a special interest. When the members of a committee of this association appeared before the Bureau of the Budget in 1928 they received a very courteous hearing. It was impossible, so the Chief of the Budget Bureau thought, to obtain all the money which the commission felt desirable; with the money which was obtained, $225,000, to be expended over a 3-year period, it was found impossible to do all the things that the committee had in mind. It was possible, however, to study those things which pertained strictly to secondary education; that is, its organization; its curriculum, including some of the more fundamental subjects, and particularly those subjects on which a comparison could be made between the present and earlier periods; its extracurriculum, which is almost entirely new in the past 30 years; the pupil population; and administrative and supervisory problems, personnel, and activities.

The handling of this Survey was intrusted to Dr. Leonard V. Koos, of the University of Chicago. With great skill he has, working on a full-time basis during his free quarters from the University of Chicago and part time during other quarters, brought it to a conclusion.

This manuscript was prepared by Ambrose Caliver, specialist in Negro education in the Office of Education, who was loaned temporarily to the research staff of the National Survey to investigate Negro education. He was assisted in the statistical work by Theresa A. Birch. The findings are most challenging. Ninety-two high schools for Negroes were reporting to the Office of Education in 1900. In 1916 Dr. Thomas Jesse Jones, who made one of the first comprehensive studies of private and higher schools for Negroes, discovered but 64 high schools in the District of Columbia and the 16 States which have separate school systems for Negroes. From that small number, only 17 years ago, there are now, roughly, 1,200 high schools for Negroes in these same States. The number of pupils has likewise increased tremendously, showing the great eagerness of the colored young people of this country for an education. In 15 Southern States with a Negro population of 9½ million, constituting 23 per cent of the total population, there are still 230 counties, in which at least one-eighth of the population is colored, which have no Negro high schools at all. This has a great bearing upon the whole problem of Negro education. In most of these States the elementary-school teachers receive their training at the present time in the high schools, so that in spite of the tremendous growth which has taken place there is still very much to be done. The matter of transporting Negro pupils to high school is a serious one. In these Southern States about two Negroes of every three live in rural areas. High schools are not close to them at best. In five States studied it is shown that for every dollar spent for the transportation of Negro pupils, $166 are spent for the transportation of white pupils. These are conditions which it will take much money to overcome. Unquestionably, the Federal Government should help with this problem.

I recommend that this manuscript be published as a monograph of the National Survey of Secondary Education.

Respectfully submitted.

WM. JOHN COOPER,
Commissioner.

The SECRETARY OF THE INTERIOR.

SECONDARY EDUCATION
FOR NEGROES

CHAPTER I : PURPOSE, SCOPE, AND PROCEDURE

1. THE NEED AND SCOPE OF THE STUDY

The problem.—The interest of the American people in education, the extent and rapid growth of education as a public enterprise, and the popularization of secondary schools in recent years are well known and are subjects of frequent comment. Less well known, however, are the interest and activity of the Negro, one of the constituent elements in American life, in education. This is particularly true with reference to education at the secondary level. It is the purpose of this report, therefore, to furnish information concerning the availability and present status of secondary education for the colored race in the Southern States.

When one considers the fact that the number of schools offering secondary work for colored children has increased from fewer than 100 to approximately 1,400 within a generation, and the more significant fact that the enrollment of Negro high-school pupils has risen, in round numbers, from 4,000 to 167,000 during the same period, the need for an investigation of the factors involved in this tremendous educational advance and of the implications of this movement becomes immediately apparent.

Receptivity of the Negro.—The influence of the educational renaissance which took place in the United States during the latter part of the eighteenth and the beginning of the nineteenth centuries vitally affected the Negro, even though he was in bondage. It aroused his imagination and fired his enthusiasm to such an extent that by emancipation a rather large number, either by stealth or through the magnanimity of their masters, had received the rudiments of education; and

[1]

it is estimated that between 5 and 10 per cent could read and write.[1]

These literate persons, some of whom were college graduates, and the contacts of the slaves with the more enlightened slaveholding class had a profound influence in stimulating a desire for education among the Negroes recently freed. Consequently, it is not strange that the need for high-school educational facilities should be felt as early as it was.

However, the economic condition of the South; general apathy, if not antagonism, against public education; prejudice against offering recently emancipated Negroes educational opportunities; and many other causes delayed the development of public educational facilities, especially of high-school grade. The development of this field was, until recent years, left almost wholly to religious and private philanthropy. As will be shown later, probably nine-tenths of the public secondary schools in the Southern States for colored youth have been organized since the beginning of the World War.

In 1900 there were 92 public high schools for Negroes reporting to the United States Bureau of Education.[2] In 1916 Thomas Jesse Jones[3] reported only 64 public high schools in the District of Columbia and the 16 States having separate school systems for the two races.

Paucity of previous information.—Until the present, little has been known regarding the number, kinds, and distribution of high schools for the Negro race, and the kind, amount, quality, and cost of these secondary-school facilities. Neither has it been known what colored boys and girls were doing with the secondary-school privileges offered them. It is the purpose of this report to throw some light on these questions, to reveal certain trends in the field of secondary education for Negroes, and to suggest the significance of some of the implication of this important movement.

Geographic region represented.—The Survey which is reported here concerned itself only with secondary education in those States having separate schools for colored and white

---

[1] Work, Monroe N. Negro Year Book, 1931–32. Tuskegee Institute, Ala., Negro Year Book Publishing Co., 1931. p. 118.

[2] U. S. Bureau of Education. Report of the Commissioner of Education, 1899–1900.

[3] Jones, Thomas Jesse. Negro Education. U. S. Bureau of Education Bulletin, 1916. No. 39.

children. Considerable effort was exerted to get information about every school doing secondary work in such States, and otherwise to learn as much as possible about the various factors entering into the secondary education of Negroes. Missouri, while not generally classified as a Southern State, is considered so in this study in light of the fact that it maintains separate schools for the two races.

2. DEVIATIONS FROM PLANS IN OTHER PORTIONS OF THE NATIONAL SURVEY

A study of status.—From what has already been said it is evident that the purpose and scope of this study is somewhat different from the larger Survey of which it is a part. The two phases differ in two important aspects. In the first place, the National Survey of Secondary Education has been "devoted chiefly to inquiries concerning efforts to improve secondary education rather than merely to a description of its present status." Studies of status have been made chiefly to provide the background against which innovating practices may be made to stand out. Inasmuch as many studies were available which furnished considerable data on the status of secondary education for white children, it was decided to have the Survey emphasize innovating and noteworthy practices as the main objective. For the section of the Survey dealing with the Negro, however, this procedure did not appear to be feasible, in view of the paucity of knowledge concerning the status of secondary education for colored children. Furthermore, the existing opinion, confirmed by the subsequent studies of the Survey, was that the progressive development of secondary education for Negroes was so recent that not enough schools could be found with modern and innovating practices to yield sufficient comparable data to make any real contribution to the advancement of secondary education for the colored race. It was decided, therefore, that the chief objective of this section of the Survey should be to ascertain status, but at the same time to collect and report all the evidence possible which would show noteworthy practices.[4]

---

[4] It is contemplated to make a subsequent report on certain outstanding features found during recent visits to Negro secondary schools.

[3]

The second important difference between the major Survey and this particular section is in their scopes. While the National Survey is, as its name implies, national in scope, it, of necessity, has gathered data largely by the selective method. It is obvious that each of the sections of the Survey, which had the responsibility of studying certain characteristic features of secondary education, could not make contact with the more than 23,000 schools, even if it were desirable.

However, in the case of this project, the total number of schools doing secondary work was small enough to make it desirable and feasible to make contact with all of them in order finally to obtain something like a representative sampling.

This special study has not precluded the participation of certain Negro schools in the general study. About 80 different forms have been sent to a large percentage of the 23,000 public high schools of the country. Thus, a few Negro schools were included among those receiving these forms. However, the Negro schools which supplied adequate data on these forms are not reported on the basis of race, but rather with respect to regional and other classifications. The data concerning them are merged with those obtained from the schools for whites.

Subjects treated.—The subjects investigated in this survey and upon which this report is based are the following: (1) Availability of secondary education for Negroes; (2) the organization of schools; (3) the Negro high-school staff; (4) Negro high-school pupils; (5) curriculum and extracurriculum offerings; (6) administration and supervision; and (7) housing and equipment.

3. THE DATA AND THEIR SOURCES

Enumeration of sources.—This particular section on Negro secondary education was begun a year after many other projects of the National Survey were under way. Because of the limited time and the nature of the objectives which this project set for itself, it was not deemed feasible to rely wholly on the data secured from the special inquiry form for Negro schools. It was decided, therefore, to use four additional agencies for collecting data on the subject, namely: (1) Reports of State superintendents and special reports from State agents or directors of Negro education; (2) regular biennial reports which are made to the statistical division of the United States Office of Education; (3) personnel blanks filled out by Negro junior and senior high school teachers for the National Survey of the Education of Teachers; and (4) personal visits. A description of these agencies follows.

Special inquiry form.—In the fall of 1930 the United States Commissioner of Education wrote the State superintendents of education in those States maintaining separate schools for the two races, explaining to them the purpose of the special study of Negro secondary education and requesting them to assist the Office in compiling a complete list of all schools in their States doing one year or more of secondary-school work, including regular 4-year public high schools, junior high schools, and private institutions. Through the cooperation of these superintendents and the State directors of Negro education a list of 1,316 schools was compiled. To the principal of each school a letter was sent explaining the nature and possible benefits of the Survey and requesting his participation.

As will be seen from Table 1, 758, or 57.6 per cent of the principals thus approached promised cooperation. To these was sent the special inquiry form concerning Negro schools. Although the form was 19 pages long, it was more of a check list than a questionnaire, as it was possible to answer most of the questions by merely checking or filling in an item.

Of the 758 principals who promised cooperation 442, or 58.3 per cent, returned the form. This is 33.5 per cent of the principals originally approached. Only 421 forms, however, were returned in time to be included in the study. These schools will hereafter be referred to as "Survey" schools. Table 1 shows the numbers and proportions of returns from each State. The 421 schools and 69,301 pupils, distributed as they are among the various States and ranging in size from the very small rural school to the large urban school, provide a fair sampling of the Negro high schools and pupils. (See Table 2.)

[5]

State reports.—The most reliable source of data regarding the availability of secondary education for Negroes was the printed reports of the State superintendents of public instruction of the 16 Southern States represented. The information secured was supplemented by facts found in special reports of directors of Negro education. Although discrepancies were found in some of these documents, they offered the most economical sources of the data desired. Much valuable information which some reports contained could not be used because all the reports were not consistent in the amount of information given, the manner of reporting, or the terminology used.

TABLE 1.—*Numbers of schools approached and numbers and percentages of secondary schools for Negroes participating in the Survey*

State	Negro high schools approached	Principals promising co-operation	Per cent (2) is of (1)	Check lists returned	Per cent (4) is of (2)	Per cent (4) is of (1)
1	2	3	4	5	6	7
Alabama	47	32	68.0	20	62.5	42.5
Arizona	1	1	100.0	1	100.0	100.0
Arkansas	72	31	43.0	15	48.4	20.8
Delaware	5	4	80.0	1	25.0	20.0
District of Columbia	13	9	69.2	5	55.5	38.4
Florida	41	20	48.7	12	60.0	29.2
Georgia	126	67	53.0	31	46.2	24.6
Illinois	11	5	45.5	2	40.0	18.1
Indiana	8	4	50.0	3	75.0	37.5
Kansas	3	3	100.0	1	33.3	33.3
Kentucky	73	38	52.0	24	63.1	32.8
Louisiana	57	46	80.7	19	41.3	33.3
Maryland	31	19	61.2	11	57.8	35.4
Mississippi	62	25	40.3	21	84.0	33.8
Missouri	42	14	33.3	13	92.8	30.7
New Jersey	3	2	66.6	0	0.0	0.0
New Mexico	3	0	0	0	0	0
North Carolina	147	83	56.4	53	63.8	36.0
Ohio	5	5	100.0	2	40.0	40.0
Oklahoma	75	42	56.0	30	71.4	40.0
Pennsylvania	3	2	66.6	1	50.0	33.3
South Carolina	80	43	53.7	25	58.1	31.2
Tennessee	71	59	83.1	40	67.8	56.3
Texas	218	112	51.3	38	33.9	12.8
Virginia	86	62	72.0	53	85.4	61.6
West Virginia	33	30	90.9	21	70.0	63.6
Total	1,316	758	57.6	442	58.3	33.5

TABLE 2.—*Numbers and percentages of schools and numbers and percentages of pupils studied by States (Survey schools)*

State	Number of schools	Per cent of total	Number of pupils	Per cent of total
1	2	3	4	5
Alabama	19	4.5	4,490	6.5
Arizona	1	.2	120	.2
Arkansas	14	3.3	2,336	3.4
Delaware	1	.2	798	1.1
District of Columbia	3	.7	2,931	4.2
Florida	9	2.1	2,095	3.0
Georgia	30	7.1	2,223	3.2
Illinois	2	.5	1,460	2.1
Indiana	3	.7	342	.5
Kansas	1	.2	573	.8
Kentucky	21	5.0	3,331	4.8
Louisiana	17	4.0	3,697	5.3
Maryland	11	2.6	5,376	7.7
Mississippi	21	5.0	1,730	2.5
Missouri	13	3.1	4,072	5.9
North Carolina	52	12.4	8,096	11.7
Ohio	2	.5	612	.9
Oklahoma	28	6.7	2,435	3.5
Pennsylvania	1	.2	114	.2
South Carolina	25	5.9	1,857	2.7
Tennessee	37	8.8	4,057	5.9
Texas	36	8.5	7,008	10.1
Virginia	52	12.4	6,912	10.0
West Virginia	22	5.2	2,636	3.8
Total	421	100.0	69,301	100.0

Statistical report forms.—Six hundred and eighty-eight schools for Negroes replied to the regular blank of inquiry sent out by the statistical division of the Office of Education requesting information for the biennium 1928–1930. These schools, hereafter to be designated "statistical" schools, furnished facts concerning length of term, enrollment, post high-school education, curriculum registration, and library facilities. Two hundred and twenty, a third of the 688 schools, also replied to the special Survey form mentioned above; this represents more than half of the 421 schools which were included in the special questionnaire study. Thus, information was obtained from a total of 875 schools. It is to be remembered, however, that in no instance is there information on any particular item for more than 421 schools; that is, the "survey" group, or 688 schools representing those in the "statistical" group. Table 3 shows the numbers and percentages of schools and the numbers and percentages of pupils in each State represented in the "statistical" group.

TABLE 3.—*Numbers and percentages of schools and numbers and percentages of students studied by States (statistical schools)*

State	Number of schools	Per cent of total	Number of pupils	Per cent of total
1	2	3	4	5
Alabama	26	3.8	6,885	6.5
Arkansas	22	3.2	2,455	2.3
Delaware	2	.3	741	.7
District of Columbia	7	1.0	6,576	6.2
Florida	22	3.2	3,095	3.0
Georgia	30	4.4	5,812	5.5
Kansas			3,163	3.0
Kentucky	59	8.6	3,493	3.3
Louisiana	6	.9	2,705	2.6
Maryland	28	4.1	6,330	6.0
Mississippi	41	5.9	3,172	3.0
Missouri	28	4.1	6,457	6.1
North Carolina	125	18.2	14,384	13.7
Oklahoma	36	5.2	4,547	4.3
South Carolina	34	4.9	3,847	3.6
Tennessee	43	6.2	6,919	6.6
Texas	130	18.9	15,096	14.3
Virginia	26	3.8	6,239	6.0
West Virginia	23	3.3	3,490	3.3
Total	688	100.0	105,406	100.0

Personnel blank.—In connection with the National Survey of the Education of Teachers [5] a personnel blank was sent to nearly a million public-school teachers. Four hundred and sixty thousand filled out and returned the blanks. Of this number 14,720 were Negro teachers, of whom 1,915 were Negro junior and senior high school teachers. Most of the data on teachers in this survey were secured from the blanks returned by these Negro junior and senior high school teachers. Although this is probably not an adequate sampling of the more than 5,000 Negro high-school teachers in the country, they are all the returns that could be secured after several follow-up efforts. In considering the data, therefore, it should be remembered that the picture presented is probably a little more favorable than is true of the typical

---

[5] This is one of the three National Surveys being made by the Office of Education. It was authorized by Congress and begun in 1930.

situation, since a large percentage of the teachers who replied were in the larger cities.

Personal visits.—In order to gain first-hand information concerning schools for Negroes, to secure knowledge that would throw light on the interpretation of the data gathered, and to assist in validating conclusions, approximately 100 schools were visited during the year 1930-31. Fifty-four of the schools visited were high schools. Also, many conferences were held with school officials, including State, city, and county superintendents; State agents and directors of Negro education; city and county supervisors; members of boards of education; and citizens.

All data for the year 1929-30.—All information secured from the various sources was for the school year 1929-30, except personnel data from the National Survey of the Education of Teachers, which were for the year 1930-31.

Comparisons for the two races.—Racial comparisons which occur frequently throughout the report have not been made with any invidious intent, but rather to throw into relief some of the conditions described and to show to what extent Negro secondary education, despite its recent progress, is behind the accepted norms as revealed by the secondary education of white children. Data on the school conditions for whites which were used for comparative purposes were secured from the following sources: Reports of State superintendents; biennial reports made to the statistical division of the Office of Education; and a special study of the smaller secondary schools made by Emery N. Ferriss, W. H. Gaumnitz, and P. Roy Brammell as a project of the National Survey of Secondary Education and published as No. 6 of the monographs of the Survey. In this connection attention should be called to the fact that although the schools comprising this last-named study are in most features similar to the Negro schools with which comparisons are made, they are predominantly located in sections other than the South, where most of the Negro schools are situated.

CHAPTER II : AVAILABILITY OF SECONDARY EDUCATION—THE GENERAL SITUATION

1. THE PROBLEM

How many Negroes of high-school age are there? How much secondary education is offered them? What kind of education is provided? What is the cost of secondary education for colored children? How available is it? To what extent are Negroes embracing the opportunities provided? These are questions which this section of the report attempts to answer.

In order to understand and appreciate the problems to be discussed, it is necessary to give consideration to the following important facts regarding the Negro in America: First, that he represents a tenth of the population of the country; second, that because of his previous condition of servitude he bears an abnormal relation to the social economy of the Nation; third, that, despite this abnormal relation, he is increasingly becoming an important and essential factor in the economic system, and an integral part of American life; and finally, as one of the constituent elements of our social order, he is required to meet without qualification all the standards of our civilization with the same degree of accuracy, speed, intelligence, and social-mindedness expected of every other citizen.

2. DESCRIPTION OF NEGRO POPULATION

According to the 1930 census there are 11,891,143 Negroes in continental United States, 9,420,747 of whom live in the Southern States represented in the investigation which have separate schools for white and colored children. This number represents 23.1 per cent of the total population in these States. Negroes living in rural sections represent 67.4 per cent of the Negro population in the same States. While the percentage of illiterate Negroes for the entire country has decreased from about 95 per cent in 1865 to 16.3 per cent in 1930, the ratio between colored and white illiteracy in the

16 Southern States studied is still very great, the percentages being 15.1 and 2.6 for Negroes and whites, respectively. Table 4 shows the population and illiteracy for each State. A fourth of the total Negro population lives in cities of 100,000 or more, the actual percentage being 24.3. This represents an increase of 6.9 per cent during the past decade.

TABLE 4.—*Total Negro population, percentage of total population in each State, percentage which is rural, and illiteracy percentages for Negroes and whites in 16 Southern States*

State	Negro population			Illiteracy	
	Number	Percentage of total for State	Percentage rural	Colored	White
1	2	3	4	5	6
Alabama	944,834	35.7	71.6	36.2	4.6
Arkansas	478,463	25.8	81.4	16.1	3.5
Florida	431,828	29.4	51.3	18.8	1.9
Georgia	1,071,125	36.8	70.4	19.9	3.3
Kentucky	226,040	8.6	48.4	15.4	5.7
Louisiana	776,326	36.9	66.8	23.3	7.3
Maryland	276,379	16.9	42.2	11.4	1.3
Mississippi	1,009,718	50.2	78.5	23.2	2.7
Missouri	223,840	6.2	24.1	8.8	1.5
North Carolina	918,647	29.0	73.2	20.6	5.6
Oklahoma	172,198	7.2	60.6	9.3	1.7
South Carolina	793,681	45.6	82.6	26.9	5.1
Tennessee	477,646	18.3	49.7	14.9	5.4
Texas	854,964	14.7	61.4	13.4	1.4
Virginia	650,165	26.8	67.2	19.2	4.8
West Virginia	114,893	6.6	72.8	11.9	3.7
Total	9,420,747	23.1	67.4	15.1	2.6

Many facts may be cited as evidence of the remarkable progress this group has made since 1865, and of the responsibility of the Nation in solving the problems which Negroes face. Some of the more important of these facts may be shown from a summary of progress of the Negro in 64 years taken from the Negro Year Book.[1] (See Table 5.)

It is estimated by Dr. Julius Klein, former Assistant Secretary of Commerce, that Negroes spend annually for food $2,200,000,000, for clothing $1,400,000,000, and for shoes $550,000,000; that they manufacture more than 60 different

---

[1] Work, Monroe N. Negro Year Book, 1931–32, p. 118.

commodities; and that there are 30,000 retail merchants among them.

These are encouraging signs, but there is also another side to the story. Some of the shadows of the picture may be observed in the following facts:

1. The life expectation of the Negro is only 45 years, as compared with 59 years for the white race.[2]

2. In 1925 the Negro death rate was 18.2 per 1,000, which was 62.5 per cent higher than the white death rate.[3]

3. The Negro infant mortality rate is approximately two-thirds above that of the whites.[4]

TABLE 5.—*Progress of the Negro in 64 years*

Types of progress	1866	1930	Gain in 64 years
1	2	3	4
Economic progress:			
Homes owned	12,000	750,000	738,000
Farms operated	20,000	1,000,000	980,000
Businesses conducted	2,100	70,000	67,900
Wealth accumulated	$20,000,000	$2,600,000,000	$2,580,000,000
Educational progress:			
Percentage literate	10	90	80
Schools for higher training [1]	15	800	785
Students in public schools	100,000	2,288,000	2,188,000
Teachers in all schools	600	56,000	55,400
Property for higher education	$60,000	$50,000,000	$49,940,000
Annual expenditures for all education	$700,000	$61,700,000	$61,000,000
Raised by Negroes	$80,000	$3,500,000	$3,420,000
Religious progress:			
Number churches	700	42,000	41,300
Communicants	600,000	5,200,000	4,600,000
Sunday schools	1,000	36,000	35,000
Sunday-school pupils	50,000	2,150,000	2,100,000
Value church property	$1,500,000	$200,000,000	$198,500,000

[1] Includes public high schools.

4. The number of Negro juvenile delinquents per 100,000 population is greater than for whites, and while both appear to be increasing the Negro rate is increasing more rapidly than the white.[5]

[2] Dublin, Louis I. The Health of the Negro. In The Negro in American Civilization, by Charles S. Johnson. New York, Henry Holt Co., 1930, p. 404.

[3] Johnson, Charles S. The Negro in American Civilization. New York, Henry Holt Co. 1930, p. 142.

[4] Ibid., p. 147.

[5] Ibid., p. 331.

5. A fourth of the Negro delinquents under 12 years studied in 1923 had not been attending school before commitment. For the whites the proportion was 6.3 per cent.

The percentage of Negro 12-year-old children not attending school was more than twice as high as the corresponding percentage of white children practically the same age; a somewhat larger percentage of white than of colored children 17 years of age were not attending. Of the Negro children 14 and 15 years of age, 2.9 per cent had never attended school, and 37.3 per cent had failed to reach the fifth grade. The corresponding percentages for white children were 0.4 and 17.4. In the age group 16 years and over, 3.8 per cent of the Negro children never attended school, and 33.1 per cent had not reached the fifth grade, the corresponding percentages for white children being 1.7 and 15.2.[6]

This brief array of important facts and characteristics regarding the life of the Negro suggests the need of more attention, with particular reference to their important implications for education.

3. THE PROPORTIONS OF THE NEGRO POPULATION OF HIGH-SCHOOL AGE ENROLLED

Comparative facts regarding the Negro population of high-school age are shown in Table 6. The percentage the high-school enrollment is of the total population of high-school age, and the percentage the high-school enrollment is of the total enrollment for Negroes and whites of high-school age in 16 States. This information is also depicted graphically in Figure 1. Attention is called to the wide differences found between the Negroes and whites in the percentage of the population of high-school age enrolled in public high schools in the various States. The range for whites is 24.5 per cent to 49.7 per cent, while for Negroes the range is 4.7 per cent to 48.9 per cent, giving a range of 25.2 per cent for whites and 44.2 per cent for Negroes. The State of Missouri furnishes the high points for both groups. In the 16 States there are 965,923 Negroes of high-school age who are not enrolled in public high schools. A few of these are, of course, enrolled in the elementary grades, and some are in private schools. However, the latter group probably constitutes a very small percentage of the total. In 1929–30 only

[6] Ibid., p. 331.

9,868 Negro private high-school pupils were reported to the Office of Education. It can conservatively be estimated that approximately 900,000 Negro boys and girls of high-school age are not in school.

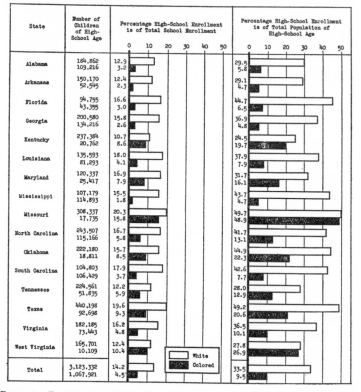

State	Number of Children of High-School Age	Percentage High-School Enrollment is of Total School Enrollment	Percentage High-School Enrollment is of Total Population of High-School Age
Alabama	184,862 / 109,216	12.9 / 3.2	29.5 / 5.8
Arkansas	150,170 / 52,545	12.4 / 2.3	29.1 / 4.7
Florida	94,755 / 43,355	16.6 / 3.0	44.7 / 6.5
Georgia	200,580 / 134,216	15.8 / 2.6	36.9 / 4.8
Kentucky	237,384 / 20,762	10.7 / 8.6	24.5 / 19.7
Louisiana	135,593 / 81,293	18.0 / 4.1	37.9 / 7.9
Maryland	120,337 / 25,417	16.9 / 7.9	31.7 / 16.1
Mississippi	107,179 / 114,893	15.5 / 1.8	43.7 / 4.7
Missouri	308,337 / 17,735	20.3 / 15.8	49.7 / 48.9
North Carolina	243,507 / 115,166	16.7 / 5.8	41.7 / 13.1
Oklahoma	222,180 / 18,811	15.7 / 8.5	44.9 / 22.3
South Carolina	104,803 / 106,429	17.9 / 3.7	42.6 / 7.7
Tennessee	224,561 / 51,835	12.2 / 5.9	28.0 / 12.9
Texas	440,198 / 92,698	19.6 / 9.3	49.2 / 20.6
Virginia	182,185 / 73,443	16.2 / 4.8	36.5 / 10.1
West Virginia	165,701 / 10,109	12.4 / 10.4	27.8 / 26.9
Total	3,123,332 / 1,067,921	14.2 / 4.5	33.5 / 9.5

White / Colored

FIGURE 1.—For 16 Southern States the number of colored and white children of high-school age and the percentages respectively of the colored and white high-school enrollment is of children of high-school age and of the total enrollment.

This great host of adolescents represents a potential source of great power and wealth for the Nation. At present it is being neglected, which makes it a readier medium for the spread of waste, inefficiency, maladjustment, disease, and crime.

Another feature of this picture to which attention should be directed is the percentage the high-school enrollment is of the total enrollment. The contrast between white and colored enrollments here also is striking, the percentages being 14.2 and 4.5, respectively. The low point for Negroes is 2.3 in Arkansas; for whites it is 10.7 in Kentucky. The high point for Negroes is 15.8 in Missouri; for whites it is 20.3 in the same State. In all States except Missouri and West Virginia the percentage the Negro high-school enrollment is of the total enrollment is less than 10, but for the white group no State falls below 10 per cent. It is clear that the percentages for Negroes lag far behind those for whites.

TABLE 6.—*Numbers in the white and colored population 15 to 19 years of age,*[1] *the percentages enrolled in high school, and the percentages the high-school enrollments are of the total enrollments*

State	Population 15 to 19 years of age [2]		Percentage high-school enrollment is of population 15 years of age		Percentage high-school enrollment is of total enrollment	
	White	Colored	White	Colored	White	Colored
1	2	3	4	5	6	7
Alabama	184,862	109,216	29.5	5.8	12.7	3.2
Arkansas	150,170	52,545	29.1	4.7	12.4	2.3
Florida	94,755	43,355	44.7	6.5	16.6	3.0
Georgia	200,580	134,216	36.9	4.8	15.8	2.6
Kentucky	237,384	20,762	24.5	19.7	10.7	8.6
Louisiana	135,593	81,293	37.9	7.9	18.5	4.1
Maryland	120,337	25,417	31.7	16.1	16.9	7.9
Mississippi	107,179	114,893	43.7	4.7	15.5	1.8
Missouri	308,337	17,735	49.7	48.9	20.3	15.8
North Carolina	243,507	115,166	41.7	13.1	16.7	5.8
Oklahoma	222,180	18,811	44.9	22.3	15.7	8.5
South Carolina	104,803	106,429	42.6	7.7	17.9	3.7
Tennessee	224,561	51,835	28.0	12.9	12.2	5.9
Texas	440,198	92,696	49.2	20.6	19.6	9.3
Virginia	182,185	73,443	36.5	10.1	16.2	4.8
West Virginia	165,701	10,109	27.8	26.9	12.4	10.4
Total	3,122,332	1,067,921	33.5	9.5	14.2	4.5

[1] The age group 15–19, inclusive, is used to represent the high-school population because they are the ages nearest those of pupils attending high school which are reported by the census according to counties. Also these ages are probably more representative of those of Negro pupils attending high school than the age group 14–17.
[2] 1930 census data.

The high-school enrollments of white and colored pupils, according to States, and the percentage each grade enrollment is of the total are shown in Table 7. In Figure 2, which represents these data graphically, one may note the zigzag nature of the profile lines for colored enrollments as compared with the almost straight lines for whites. The enrollment percentages in the various grades for white pupils vary hardly more than 1 per cent in the different

[15]

States. For colored pupils the percentages grade enrollments are of total enrollments have the following ranges: Fourth year, 6.1 to 15.3; third year, 10.6 to 20.6; second year, 24.4 to 31.2; and for the first year, 34.3 to 56.5. Atten-

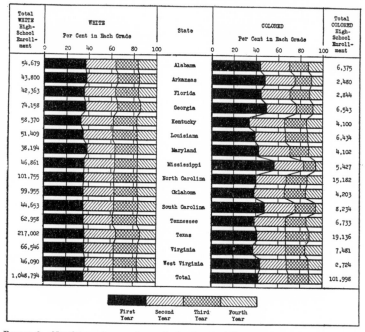

FIGURE 2.—Numbers and percentages of colored and white pupils enrolled in public high schools, by years, in 15 Southern States, 1930

tion is called particularly to the contrast between the colored and white enrollments for the first and fourth years. The lengths of the ranges of enrollments in each grade for white and colored pupils are, respectively: First year, 5.6 and 22.2; second year, 3.5 and 6.8; third year, 2.9 and 10; fourth year, 2.9 and 9.2. While these percentages do not present an absolutely true picture of the high-school pupil mortality, they may be assumed to be at least approximate measures of the elimination and survival of pupils.

A detailed analysis of this problem in a particular State or several States covering a period of four years, and a study of factors influencing the variation in pupil mortality in different States, offer fruitful fields for further investigation.

TABLE 7.—*Numbers and percentages of white and colored pupils enrolled in public high schools, by years, in 15 Southern States, 1930*

State	White pupils enrolled in high school, by grades					Colored pupils enrolled in high school, by grades				
	First year	Second year	Third year	Fourth year	Total	First year	Second year	Third year	Fourth year	Total
1	2	3	4	5	6	7	8	9	10	11
Alabama:										
Number	20,242	13,822	10,680	8,935	54,679	2,796	1,714	1,041	824	6,375
Per cent	37.0	27.1	19.5	16.3		43.8	26.8	16.3	12.9	
Arkansas:										
Number	16,701	12,093	8,254	6,752	43,800	1,188	685	358	249	$2,480
Per cent	38.1	27.6	18.8	15.4		47.9	27.6	14.4	10.0	
Florida:										
Number	15,356	11,689	8,566	6,662	42,363	1,262	755	488	339	2,844
Per cent	36.2	27.6	20.2	15.9		44.4	26.5	17.2	11.9	
Georgia:										
Number	27,704	21,113	14,926	10,415	74,158	3,223	1,780	953	587	6,543
Per cent	37.3	28.4	20.1	14.0		49.3	27.2	14.6	8.9	
Kentucky:										
Number	19,199	16,983	12,275	9,913	58,370	1,407	1,279	814	600	4,100
Per cent	32.9	29.1	21.0	16.9		34.3	31.2	19.8	14.6	
Louisiana:										
Number	17,957	13,760	11,142	8,550	51,409	2,537	1,755	1,263	879	6,434
Per cent	34.9	26.8	21.7	16.6		39.4	27.3	19.6	13.7	
Maryland:										
Number	14,691	9,765	7,601	6,137	38,194	1,728	1,158	699	517	4,102
Per cent	38.5	25.6	19.9	16.0		43.1	28.2	17.0	12.6	
Mississippi:										
Number	16,987	12,882	9,432	7,560	46,861	3,066	1,448	579	334	5,427
Per cent	36.2	27.5	20.1	16.1		56.5	26.7	10.6	6.1	
North Carolina:										
Number	36,789	27,271	21,182	16,513	101,755	6,110	4,175	2,783	2,114	15,182
Per cent	36.1	26.8	20.8	16.2		40.2	27.5	18.3	13.9	

[17]

TABLE 7.—*Numbers and percentages of white and colored pupils enrolled in public high schools, by years, in 15 Southern States, 1930*—Continued

State	White pupils enrolled in high school, by grades					Colored pupils enrolled in high school, by grades				
	First year	Second year	Third year	Fourth year	Total	First year	Second year	Third year	Fourth year	Total
1	2	3	4	5	6	7	8	9	10	11
Oklahoma:										
Number	35,443	27,261	21,028	16,224	99,956	1,620	1,150	787	646	4,203
Per cent	35.4	27.3	21.0	16.2		38.5	27.4	18.7	15.3	
South Carolina:										
Number	16,047	12,010	9,527	7,069	44,653	3,980	2,312	1,407	535	8,234
Per cent	35.9	26.9	21.3	15.8		48.3	28.1	17.1	6.5	
Tennessee:										
Number	22,296	16,693	13,496	10,473	62,958	2,628	1,879	1,263	963	6,733
Per cent	35.4	26.5	21.4	16.6		39.0	27.9	18.7	14.3	
Texas:										
Number	79,512	62,090	44,493	30,907	217,002	7,964	4,988	3,949	2,235	19,136
Per cent	36.6	28.6	20.5	14.2		42.1	26.1	20.6	11.7	
Virginia:										
Number	23,808	18,137	14,444	10,157	66,546	2,844	2,264	1,229	1,144	7,481
Per cent	35.8	27.2	21.7	15.3		38.0	30.3	16.4	15.3	
West Virginia:										
Number	17,181	12,091	9,292	7,526	46,090	1,199	666	510	349	2,724
Per cent	37.3	26.2	20.2	16.3		44.0	24.4	18.7	12.8	
Total:										
Number	379,913	288,660	216,338	163,883	1,048,794	43,552	28,008	18,123	12,315	101,998
Per cent	36.2	27.5	20.6	15.6		42.7	27.4	17.8	12.1	

4. A MEASURE OF THE AVAILABILITY OF SECONDARY EDUCATION

As previously mentioned, there are approximately 1,000,000 Negro children of high-school age in the 15 States in which this special study was made. Of this number slightly more than 100,000 are enrolled in public high schools. One

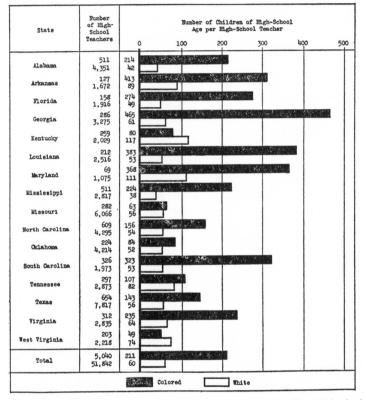

State	Number of High-School Teachers	Number of Children of High-School Age per High-School Teacher
Alabama	511 / 4,351	214 / 42
Arkansas	127 / 1,672	413 / 89
Florida	158 / 1,916	274 / 49
Georgia	286 / 3,275	465 / 61
Kentucky	259 / 2,029	80 / 117
Louisiana	212 / 2,516	383 / 53
Maryland	69 / 1,075	368 / 111
Mississippi	511 / 2,817	224 / 38
Missouri	282 / 6,066	63 / 56
North Carolina	609 / 4,295	156 / 54
Oklahoma	224 / 4,214	84 / 52
South Carolina	326 / 1,973	323 / 53
Tennessee	297 / 2,873	107 / 82
Texas	654 / 7,817	143 / 56
Virginia	312 / 2,835	235 / 64
West Virginia	203 / 2,218	49 / 74
Total	5,040 / 51,842	211 / 60

Colored   White

FIGURE 3.—Number of high-school teachers and number of high-school pupils per high-school teacher in 16 Southern States, according to race

measure of the availability of secondary education to these 1,000,000 children is the ratio between the total number of children of high-school age and the number of high-school teachers. This is shown in Figure 3. The diagram gives the number of high-school teachers and the number of persons of high-school age per high-school teacher for the white and colored races by States.

In this discussion it is assumed that persons of high-school age per teacher offers a better index of availability of secondary education for Negroes than high-school pupils per teacher. This discussion is concerned with opportunites offered potential pupils as well as those actually enrolled. There is considerable evidence to show that enrollment tends to increase in direct proportion to the educational facilities afforded by a State or community.

In the 16 States under investigation, according to reports of the State departments of education for 1930, there were 51,842 white high-school teachers and 5,040 colored high-school teachers. This gives 60 potential pupils for each white teacher to teach or influence and 211 for each colored teacher.

5. PER PUPIL COST OF SECONDARY EDUCATION

Another index of the amount, and to some extent of the quality, of education offered pupils is in terms of its cost. The amount of money a State or community spends for education not only limits the number of teachers and the amount of equipment available but it also determines the quality.

The amount spent by 10 States for high-school teachers' salaries and the cost of teachers' salaries per high-school pupil and per person of high-school age are represented in Figure 4. Again both pupil and potential pupil have been used in attempting to determine the index of opportunity or availability. It will be noted that the differential in every State between whites and Negroes is far greater in cost per person of high-school age than in the cost per high-school pupil.

Two features of this diagram are worthy of note: First, in only two States is the cost per pupil twice as great for whites as for Negroes; while in seven States the cost per person of high-school age ranged from six to thirteen times greater for whites than for Negroes. The second feature to which attention is directed is the approximate equality of expenditures in the States of Kentucky and West Virginia. In Kentucky the

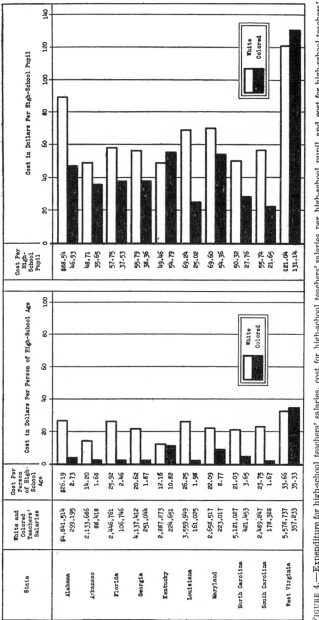

FIGURE 4.—Expenditure for high-school teachers' salaries, cost for high-school teachers' salaries per high-school pupil, and cost for high-school teachers' salaries per child of high-school age in 10 Southern States, according to race

expenditure per Negro high-school pupil exceeds that for whites. This is also true of West Virginia for both high-school pupils and potential pupils.

6. OTHER COSTS

Data for certain States on the cost of operation, maintenance, transportation, and library are presented in Table 8. In view of the importance of transportation in the development of consolidated high schools it is of interest to note the total amount spent in six States for the transportation of high-school pupils for the year 1930. For Negro children the expenditure was $30,189; for white children it amounted to $5,594,942. Facts regarding the library are also illuminating in their revelation of the amount and kind of education afforded colored children through this medium. Expenditures for libraries in Negro schools range from $80 to $1,374; for white schools in the same States it is from $15,138 to $54,099.

TABLE 8.—*Expenditures for operation, maintenance, transportation, and libraries in high schools for white and colored pupils in certain Southern States, 1930*

State	Cost of operation of high schools		Cost of maintenance of high schools		Cost of transportation of high-school students		Expenditure for library		Number of volumes of books in library	
	White	Colored	White	Colored	White	Colored	White	Colored	White	Colored
1	2	3	4	5	6	7	8	9	10	11
Alabama	$265,354	$15,674	$197,995	$11,624	$612,494	$1,897	$54,099	$820		
Arkansas [1]	174,174	8,238	87,753	3,851						
Florida	[2]829,898	[2]75,995	[2]377,456	[2]47,090	1,020,819	10,949	[2]21,764	[2]80		
Georgia	[2]578,764	[2]63,873	[2]413,873	[2]49,880	1,053,649	200	[2]40,324	[2]670	591,300	25,228
Louisiana	836,985	106,973	844,836	114,582						
Maryland	290,086	37,213	145,750	9,746	1,913,195	16,087	[3]44,866	[3]1,374	[3]1,061,827	[3]91,499
North Carolina	1,548,518	216,498	732,197	93,965					449,823	8,840
Oklahoma									163,682	9,782
South Carolina [4]	193,110	10,908	60,264	2,541	455,689		15,138	223		
Texas					539,096	1,056				
West Virginia									372,389	23,524
Total	4,716,889	535,372	2,860,124	333,279	5,594,942	30,189	176,191	3,167	2,639,021	158,873

[1] 1927–28 data.　　[2] For all grades, both elementary and high school.　　[3] 1928–29 data.　　[4] 1931 data.

[23]

1. THE NUMBER OF SCHOOLS

How many schools are there in the States maintaining dual systems which offer high-school work for colored children? What kinds of schools are they? How many years of secondary work do they offer? Answers to these questions may be found in Table 9.

In studying this table attention should be called to certain possible inaccuracies. In the first place, there is reason to believe that not all private schools were reported for the States represented. Whenever possible, these omissions were supplied. Secondly, a few cases of omissions of public schools were found. Whenever possible, these, too, were added. Third, the fact that there are frequent changes from year to year in the number of years of secondary work offered by individual schools makes it difficult to report with absolute accuracy. These changes often result from lack of teachers, insufficient funds, or lack of pupils registering (and prepared) for certain years of high-school work.

Reports were corrected in some places by adding a school to the count where public high school pupils were reported for certain counties and no high school indica ;ed. As explained in the first chapter, the State departments were requested to list all schools doing any amount of high-school work of one or more years. In addition, careful study was made of biennial reports of State superintendents. It is believed that Table 9, drawn from a combination of these two sources, presents as accurate a picture of the situation as was obtainable under the circumstances.

In this particular investigation only the last four years of high school were considered. In the case of junior high schools in States having the 12-year system the ninth grade was taken as the first year of high school. In States having the 11-grade system the eighth grade was considered the first year.

TABLE 9.—*Number of public and private high schools for colored children in 15 Southern States,[1] 1929-30, including the numbers of rural and urban high schools offering the different years of work*

State	Number of 4-year high schools			4-year accredited high schools			Number of public high schools, by years, offered and by location								Total
							Rural				Urban				
	Public	Private	Total	Public	Private	Total	One	Two	Three	Four	One	Two	Three	Four	
1	2	3	4	5	6	7	8	9	10	11	12	13	14	15	16
Alabama	33	10	43	7	10	17	61	10	15	23	13	4	2	10	138
Arkansas[2]	12	5	17	1	3	4	24	9	5	3	10	3	3	9	66
Florida	22	5	27	14	3	17					24			22	46
Georgia[3]	32	17	49	14	14	28		[4]45		10		[4]32		22	109
Kentucky	40	3	43	19	3	22	1	10	3	10	2	5	5	30	66
Louisiana[3,5]	29	13	42	4	6	10	1							17	38
Maryland	14		14	14		14	1	5	2	12	3	2	7	1	29
Mississippi[6]	14	14	28	13	14	27	2	12	6	13	4	15	1	12	39
Missouri	16		16	11		11		4	5	2	2	7	3	16	42
North Carolina	72	20	92	68	20	88	18	17	11	29	6		4	43	135
Oklahoma	37		37	18		18	9	16	6	24	1	3		13	72
Tennessee	27	4	31	17	4	21		24	4	21			1	6	56
Texas[3]	85	8	93	26	8	34	7	30	55	21	2	6	25	64	210
Virginia[7]	45	13	58	18	9	27	4	12	9	32		1		13	71
West Virginia	28		28								5			28	33
Total	506	112	618	244	94	338	128	194	121	200	72	78	51	306	[8]1,150

[1] These data were obtained from reports of State superintendents and State agents for Negro schools.
[2] 1929-30 data.
[3] All schools in places of 2,500 population or less considered as rural.
[4] Listed as 2-year or 3-year schools.
[5] 4 additional new training schools; number of years not designated.
[6] 7 additional county training schools; number of years not designated.
[7] Data from 1930-31 State list of schools.
[8] 54 schools gave insufficient information for classification.

It will be noted that there is a total of 618 4-year high schools reported. Five hundred and six of these are public and 112 are private schools. From the sources investigated there appear also to be 644 other schools offering varying amounts of secondary work. Four hundred and forty-three of these were rural and 201 urban schools. In cases where the report did not designate the kind of school—that is, whether rural or urban—reference was made to the 1930 census report and all schools located in communities of 2,500 or fewer were classed as rural. It is significant of mention that although 67.4 per cent of the Negro population of these States is rural only 39 per cent of the 4-year public high schools are available to them. This table, studied in connection with Figures 2 and 3 will reveal some interesting tendencies relating to the ratio between the Negro population of high-school age enrolled and number and kinds of high schools and teachers available. The enrollment appears to increase in direct ratio to the number of schools and teachers per population.

Another important feature of this table is the number of schools reported to be accredited. Of the 101,998 Negro boys and girls attending public high schools in the States included, only a small percentage have access to an approved secondary school. Only 244, or less than half, of the public 4-year schools are reported as being accredited by the State department of education.[1] The implications of this fact are highly important and far reaching. Nearly 84 per cent of the 112 private high schools listed are accredited.

2. COUNTIES HAVING NO 4-YEAR HIGH SCHOOLS

In order to ascertain further the availability of secondary-school facilities for Negroes, a study was made similar to the one reported by L. M. Favrot in 1928.[2] Investigation was made of all counties where Negroes represent 12½ per cent or more of the population in 15 Southern States. These counties were divided into three groups, as follows: Group A, counties having a Negro population of 12½ to 25 per cent of

---

[1] Until recently only a few Negro high schools could gain accreditment by any of the national and regional accrediting organizations. A year ago the Southern Association of Colleges and Secondary Schools undertook to accredit Negro high schools. Up to and including December, 1932, this Association had accredited 36 high schools for Negroes, 21 public and 15 private.

[2] Favrot, Leo M. Some Facts About Negro High Schools and Their Distribution and Development in 14 Southern States. High-School Quarterly, 17 : 139-154, April, 1929.

the total population; Group B, counties having a Negro population of 26 to 50 per cent; and Group C, counties having a Negro population of 51 per cent or more. These counties were studied with respect to the presence or absence of public high schools for Negroes. The data were secured from the same sources used in the investigation described in the preceding section.

The results of this study by States are given in Table 10. A detailed analysis being inexpedient, it must suffice to call attention here to the facts revealed in the total situation. There are 56 counties in Group A without any 4-year high school facilities for colored children. These counties have a Negro population of 244,871, including 28,605 Negro children of high-school age. There are 88 Group B counties without fourth-year facilities. In these counties there is a total of 667,951 colored people, 78,641 of whom are of high-school age. The Group C counties total 51. They represent approximately three-fourths of a million Negroes and 89,996 colored persons of high-school age who do not have the privilege of four years of secondary schooling.

The total number of counties in these States with no 4-year high-school facilities for colored children is 195, representing a Negro population of 1,671,501, and 197,242 persons of high-school age. This number is 20.5 per cent of the total Negro population of high-school age in the 15 States studied.

3. COUNTIES WITHOUT HIGH-SCHOOL FACILITIES

The large number of colored children deprived of four years of secondary schooling may have impressed the reader with the seriousness of some of the educational problems confronting certain States. Of far greater importance, however, is the situation concerning the number of colored children without the privilege of attending any public high school of any kind unless they leave the counties in which they reside. The data bearing on this situation are shown in Table 11.

In the 15 States comprising this investigation, 230 counties, with a Negro population of 12½ per cent or more of the total, are without high-school facilities for colored children. These counties contain 1,397,304 colored people, 158,939 of whom are 15 to 19 years of age. These young people represent 16.5

TABLE 10.—*Counties having less than four years of high-school work for Negroes where they represent 12.5 per cent or more of the population, 1930* [1]

State	A. Counties with Negro population 12½ to 25 per cent of total population			B. Counties with Negro population 26 to 50 per cent of total population			C. Counties with Negro population 51 per cent and more of total population			Total number of counties	Total Negro population	Total persons of high-school age without 4-year high-school facilities	
	Number of counties	Negro population	Population of high-school age	Number of counties	Negro population	Population of high-school age	Number of counties	Negro population	Population of high-school age			Number	Per centage of total having some high-school facilities
1	2	3	4	5	6	7	8	9	10	11	12	13	14
Alabama	9	58,908	7,339	4	73,761	8,139	9	182,280	22,705	22	314,949	38,183	37.8
Arkansas	5	19,752	2,169	13	125,592	14,493	4	55,903	5,806	22	201,247	22,468	52.9
Florida	1	10,974	1,061	2	8,911	896				3	19,885	1,957	6.3
Georgia	10	45,850	6,022	22	132,065	17,722	20	160,804	20,924	52	338,719	44,668	41.9
Kentucky	5	12,232	1,262							5	12,232	1,262	6.1
Louisiana	3	11,038	1,105	2	23,673	2,531	2	31,051	3,155	7	65,762	6,791	11.1
Maryland	1	8,266	873	3	15,610	1,847				4	23,876	2,720	11.2
Mississippi	3	8,283	887	14	137,218	13,362	11	269,359	30,964	28	414,860	45,213	59.3
Missouri	1	1,937	172	1	10,040	1,013				2	11,977	1,185	6.9
North Carolina	2	4,851	675	6	30,055	3,889	1	10,799	1,476	9	45,705	6,040	5.7
Oklahoma	1	4,994	595							1	4,994	595	3.2
Tennessee	4	18,597	2,132	1	8,532	1,012	1	21,095	2,766	6	48,224	5,910	11.9
Texas	7	27,877	3,059	12	73,123	8,770	1	5,117	638	20	106,117	12,467	15.3
Virginia	4	11,312	1,254	8	39,371	4,967	2	12,271	1,562	14	62,954	7,783	16.1
Total	56	244,871	28,605	88	677,951	78,641	51	748,679	89,996	195	1,671,501	197,242	24.5

[1] South Carolina was omitted from this study, as it was not possible to ascertain the number of years offered by the high schools in each county. However, Negro high-school pupils are reported from every county in the State, making a total of 8,945.

[28]

TABLE 11.—*Counties without provision of high-school work for Negroes where they represent 12.5 per cent or more of the population, 1930* [1]

State	A. Counties with Negro population 12½ to 25 per cent of total population			B. Counties with Negro population 26 to 50 per cent of total population			C. Counties with Negro population 51 per cent and more of total population			Total number counties	Total Negro population	Total persons of high-school age without high-school facilities	
	Number counties	Negro population	Population of high-school age	Number counties	Negro population	Population of high-school age	Number counties	Negro population	Population of high-school age			Number	Per-cent-age
	2	3	4	5	6	7	8	9	10	11	12	13	14
Alabama	3	15,465	1,777	4	41,255	5,071	1	10,789	1,407	8	67,509	8,255	7.5
Arkansas	2	8,157	896	3	26,481	3,292	2	53,851	5,903	7	88,489	10,091	19.2
Florida	11	28,089	2,822	26	84,076	8,847	1	8,203	1,032	38 [2]	120,368	12,701	29.2
Georgia	10	24,358	3,173	27	121,401	15,734	12	66,022	8,843	49	211,781	27,750	20.6
Kentucky	1	1,200	108							1	1,200	108	.5
Louisiana	8	36,701	3,930	14	86,512	9,273	6	68,963	7,144	28	192,176	20,347	25.0
Maryland	2	7,293	699	1	5,592	638				3	12,885	1,337	5.2
Mississippi	10	33,129	3,796	14	107,102	12,727	15	190,257	22,161	39	330,488	38,684	33.6
Missouri	1	5,617	633							1	5,617	633	3.5
North Carolina	2	7,788	1,012	8	63,460	8,153	1	8,635	1,248	11	79,883	10,413	9.0
Tennessee	3	7,206	920	2	11,317	1,449				5	18,523	2,369	4.5
Texas	2	3,324	353	2	6,659	774				4	9,983	1,127	1.4
Virginia	14	42,446	4,602	19	204,997	19,178	3	10,959	1,344	36	258,402	25,124	34.2
Total	69	220,773	24,721	120	758,852	85,136	41	417,679	49,082	230	1,397,304	158,939	16.5

[1] Oklahoma and West Virginia are omitted from this table, as they have no counties with 12½ per cent Negro population or more without high-school facilities.

[2] Four counties report students but no high schools.

per cent of all Negroes between the ages of 15 and 19 in the 15 Southern States represented. The 230 counties studied, their total Negro population, and population of high-school age are distributed as follows: Group A, 69 counties, 220,773 Negro population, 24,721 population 15 to 19 years of age; Group B, 120 counties, 758,852 Negro population, 85,136 population 15 to 19 years of age; and Group C, 41 counties, 417,679 Negro population, 49,082 population 15 to 19 years of age.

To offset the possible assumption that many of the counties, particularly in Group A, have a small total population and consequently few Negroes, an investigation of this item was made, resulting in the discovery that in no case did the Negro population of high-school age fall below 60. There are 11 counties with 60 to 100 Negroes of high-school age; 32 counties with 101 to 200; and 53 with 201 to 300. In each of the other of the 230 counties without any high-school facilities for the colored race there are more than 300 Negroes 15 to 19 years of age. Figure 5 presents a summary of this discussion in tabular and graphic form.

4. SUMMARY

The Negro population of the specific States under consideration is 9,420,747, or 23.1 per cent of the total population. Sixty-seven and four-tenths per cent of this number reside in rural sections, and 15.1 per cent above 10 years of age are illiterate, as compared with 2.6 per cent of the white population in the same States. Approximately a tenth, or 1,067,921 of these colored persons, are of high-school age, but only 9.5 per cent of these potential pupils are in public high schools. Of the 3,123,332 white persons of high school age 33.5 per cent in the same States are enrolled in public high schools.

Five hundred and six public 4-year high schools are provided for these 1,000,000 Negroes 15 to 19 years of age. The enrollment in these schools is 101,998, 42.7 per cent of whom are in the first year, 27.4 per cent in the second year, 17.8 per cent in the third year, and only 12.1 per cent in the fourth year. The percentage the high-school enrollment is of the total enrollment is 14.2 for whites and 4.5 for Negroes.

The number of persons of high-school age per high-school teacher ranges from 49 to 465 for Negroes, and from 38 to 117 for whites, the extent of the range for Negroes being 426 per cent greater than for whites. Marked differences between the two races are also found in the expenditures for teachers' salaries per high-school pupil and per person of high-school age, and likewise in the costs for operation, maintenance, transportation, and library.

FIGURE 5.—Percentage of Negro population of high-school age in 15 Southern States without 4-year high-school facilities and percentage having no high-school facilities

If the 230 counties which have no high schools at all for Negroes and the 195 having no 4-year high schools are combined, we have a total of 425, which is 30 per cent of the 1,413 counties in the States under investigation. In each of the 425 counties Negroes represent 12.5 per cent or more of the population, and in every case the total Negro population of high-school age exceeds 60 in number.

CHAPTER IV : THE ORGANIZATION OF SCHOOLS

1. DISTRIBUTION OF SCHOOLS AND PUPILS

In Chapters II and III a general overview was given of the availability of secondary-school facilities for Negroes in 16 Southern States. Facts regarding the complete situation with respect to several important factors and characteristics were presented. The status of the facilities provided will now be presented by studying the characteristic features of a sampling of schools and their staffs. The schools will not only be studied by States, but also by size, type, and kind.

For purposes of comparison the 407 [1] schools replying to the Special Survey inquiry form have been classified into six groups comprising the following enrollments: Group I, 40 or fewer; Group II, 41–75; Group III, 76–150; Group IV, 151–300; Group V, 301–500; and Group VI, 501 or more. The 688 schools replying to the biennial inquiry of the statistical division which were also used in this Survey had been classified according to another grouping. They were, therefore, regrouped to correspond as nearly as possible to the groups used for the regular Survey forms. The groups are designated by letters, the A group corresponding to Group I, B to Group II, and so on. The enrollments in these groups are as follows: Group A, 10–49; Group B, 50–74; Group C, 75–199; Group D, 200–299; Group E, 300-499; Group F, 500 or more. (See Tables 12 and 13.)

As stated in the first chapter, the schools responding to the special inquiry form for the Negro secondary schools are referred to in this report as the "Survey" schools, and the schools which filled out and returned to the statistical division the regular biennial statistical report as the "statistical" schools. In both the Survey and statistical schools, those reported as regular 4-year high schools, or which are operating on the 8-4 plan, were classified as regular, while all

---

[1] 14 schools did not give enrollments, so could not be grouped according to size.

others were classed as reorganized. Of the Survey schools, 215, or 52.8 per cent, offer a 4-year program.

The distribution of the 407 Survey schools according to the number of schools and pupils belonging to the various size groups, types, and kinds is shown in Table 12. The total number of pupils enrolled in these schools, according to the replies, is 69,301. The percentages of schools and the percentages of pupils belonging to the various size groups are in inverse ratio to each other. Although 30.9 per cent of the 407 schools belong to Group I, these schools enroll only 4.3 per cent of the pupils. Similarly, Group VI contains only 8.3 per cent of the schools, but 50.3 per cent of the pupils.

TABLE 12.—*Numbers and percentages of schools and numbers and percentages of pupils studied by size, type, and kind of school (Survey group)*

Grouping	Number of schools	Percentage of total	Number of pupils	Percentage of total
1	2	3	4	5
Size group:				
I (40 or fewer)	126	31.0	3,015	4.3
II (41–75)	86	21.1	4,816	7.0
III (76–150)	101	25.0	10,513	15.1
IV (151–300)	43	10.5	9,254	13.3
V (301–500)	17	4.1	6,842	10.0
VI (501 or more)	34	8.3	34,861	50.3
Total	407	100.0	69,301	100.0
Type:				
Regular	313	74.3	42,117	60.7
Reorganized	108	25.6	27,184	39.2
Total	[1] 421	100.0	69,301	100.0
Kind:				
Public	239	56.0	55,725	80.5
Private	48	11.0	4,501	6.4
County training school [2]	131	31.0	8,646	12.5
Combination of kinds	3	1.0	429	.6
Total	[1] 421	100.0	69,301	100.0

[1] Includes 14 schools not grouped by size.
[2] Public schools. One of the most important recent developments in Negro education has been the growth of county training schools, made possible by the cooperation of the county school authorities and the John F. Slater Fund. A study of these high schools, made by L. M. Favrot, will be found in Occasional Papers No. 23 of the John F. Slater Fund, Washington, D. C., 1923. Other references to them will be found in Occasional Papers Nos. 14 and 18 and the 1929 report of the Slater Fund.

The distribution of the 688 statistical schools by size groups, type, and size of place is shown in Table 13. It will be observed that the tendencies in Groups I and VI correspond closely to those found in Table 12, but in Groups II, III, IV, and V there is considerable fluctuation.

The regular schools constitute 74.3 per cent of the total number with 60.7 per cent of the enrollment, while 25.6 per cent of the schools are reorganized, enrolling 39.2 per cent of the pupils.

TABLE 13.—*Numbers and percentages of schools and numbers and percentages of pupils studied by size of place, and by type and size of school (statistical group)*

Grouping	Number of schools	Percentage of total	Number of pupils	Percentage of total
1	2	3	4	5
Size of place:				
100,000 or more	41	6.0	35,537	36.0
30,000–99,999	43	6.0	15,880	16.0
10,000–29,999	100	15.0	16,951	17.0
2,500–9,999	224	32.4	15,951	16.0
Fewer than 2,500	280	40.6	14,774	15.0
Total	688	100.0	[1] 99,093	100.0
Type:				
Reorganized	149	21.6	45,333	43.0
Regular	539	78.3	60,073	56.9
Total	688	100.0	105,406	100.0
Size of school:				
A (10–49)	294	42.7	8,277	8.0
B (50–74)	93	13.5	5,679	5.3
C (75–199)	193	28.0	23,410	22.2
D (200–299)	38	5.5	9,371	9.0
E (300–499)	27	3.1	11,162	10.5
F (500 or more)	43	6.2	47,507	45.0
Total	688	100.0	105,406	100.0

[1] Information reported from enrollment by curriculums.

2. TYPES OF DISTRICTS

The types of districts under which the Survey schools operate are as follows: City, 220; county, 129; district consolidated, 33; open country, 6 [2]; other, 33; total, 421.

3. ACCESSIBILITY OF SCHOOLS

Some indication of how accessible these schools are to the pupils who attend them is given in Table 14. Of the 239 schools reporting on this item, 72 (or 30 per cent) served an

[2] 74 other schools which were in the open country also reported some other type of district organization. These are distributed to the county, district-consolidated, and other groups.

area each of more than 30 square miles, while only 55 schools (or 23 per cent) served an area as small as 5 square miles. Districts of this smaller area would afford convenient walking distances. These facts have considerable significance when it is remembered that transportation facilities are very infrequently provided for colored children. From the data studied there appears to be little variation in this factor with respect to the sizes of schools.

It is realized that this is a crude measure of accessibility. Yet it gives some idea of the distances children are from school. In many rural counties only a single school exists for the colored children, and frequently the counties are hundreds of square miles in area and the Negro population is often widely scattered over the county. This question, in reference to the density and sparsity of the Negro population, should receive further study in order that a more accurate conclusion in the matter may be derived.

TABLE 14.—*Numbers and percentages of Negro high schools serving districts of given sizes, by size of school*

Area of district in square miles	Size groups						Total schools reply-ing
	I	II	III	IV	V	VI	
1	2	3	4	5	6	7	8
5 or less:							
Number	22	8	12	8	2	3	55
Per cent	27.5	17.3	22.2	28.5	22.2	13.6	23.0
6 to 10:							
Number	14	10	12	6	3	4	49
Per cent	17.5	21.6	22.2	21.4	33.3	18.1	20.5
11 to 20:							
Number	11	11	10	5	3	3	43
Per cent	13.7	23.9	18.5	17.8	33.3	13.6	17.9
21 to 30:							
Number	10	4	3	1		2	20
Per cent	12.5	8.6	5.5	3.5		9.0	8.3
More than 30:							
Number	23	13	17	8	1	10	72
Per cent	28.7	28.2	31.4	28.5	11.1	45.4	30.1
Total schools replying	80	46	54	28	9	22	239
Per cent each total is of all schools in group	63.4	53.4	53.4	65.1	52.9	64.7	58.7

4. DISTRIBUTION OF SCHOOLS BY SIZE OF STAFF

The size of the teaching staff is an important index of the extent of educational opportunity a school offers its pupils.

One-, two-, and three-teacher schools may be unsatisfactory for the elementary grades, but they are worse for high-school grades. The difficulty and specialization of the subject matter in the high school involves a variety and a complexity of problems which are not encountered in the lower grades. It is of significance, therefore, that attention be called to the large percentage of Negro high schools with small teaching forces. Of the 421 Survey schools replying to this query, 187 (or 45.5 per cent) had from one to three teachers only. Of the 490 unselected 4-year white high schools only 21.2 per cent had so few as three teachers. Only 16 per cent of the Negro schools had more than 10 teachers as compared with 37 per cent for the white group.[3]

5. DATES OF ESTABLISHMENT AND ACCREDITMENT OF SCHOOLS

Another important factor influencing the popularization of secondary education for Negroes is the length of time high-school work has been offered in a given community. Figure 6 gives a picture of trends in the establishment of Negro high schools. In addition, it shows trends in the offering of a full 4-year program and accreditment. Three features of this diagram are worthy of note: First, 68 per cent of the 299 schools replying to this question began offering high-school work after the beginning of the World War; second, of the 240 schools replying to the question relating to a full 4-year program, 80 per cent answered that they had begun the practice some time since 1915; third, of the 218 schools replying to the accreditment question, 86 per cent answered that they had received accreditment since 1920.

These trends correspond closely to certain other facts revealed in the study of availability, where it was shown that only 338 colored schools were reported by the State departments of 15 States as having an accredited status, and that 94 of these were private schools.

According to the study of the smaller secondary school,[4] of 379 schools replying to the question concerning organization of high-school work, 85.5 per cent had begun before 1921. Of

[3] Ferriss, Emery N., Gaumnitz, W. H., and Brammell, P. Roy. The Smaller Secondary Schools. In National Survey of Secondary Education. Washington, Government Printing Office, 1933. (Bulletin, 1932, No. 17, Monograph No. 6.)
[4] Ibid.

the 4-year unselected white high schools in the same study only 57 per cent received accreditment after 1921. This is in sharp contrast to the corresponding percentage for colored schools, which is 86.

6. LENGTH OF TERM

The length of term is an important index of the amount of educational opportunity being provided. In this regard the high schools for colored pupils do not suffer greatly in comparison with the high schools for whites, a close correlation existing between both ranges of term length in days and medians for the two groups in the three criteria, type of school size group, and size of community.

7. SUMMARY

The Negro high schools are in general of recent development, and many are inaccessible to the constituency they are intended to serve. Most of them began offering a 4-year program since 1915; practically all having an accredited status have received accreditment since 1920.

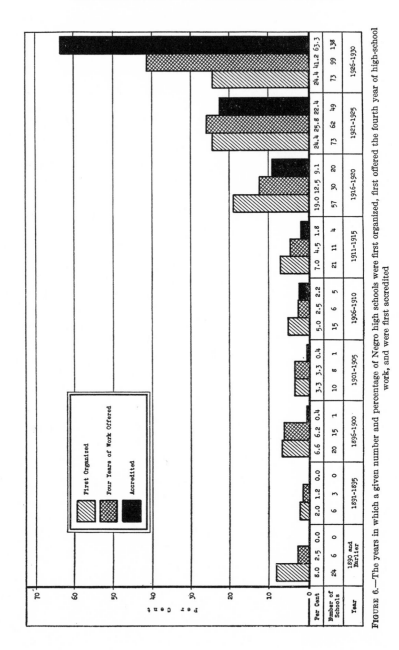

FIGURE 6.—The years in which a given number and percentage of Negro high schools were first organized, first offered the fourth year of high-school work, and were first accredited

CHAPTER V : THE HIGH-SCHOOL OFFERING

1. THE PROGRAM OF STUDIES

In the previous chapter certain features of the external organization and administration of Negro high schools were discussed. It will be the concern of this chapter to set forth two of the important features of the internal operation of the schools, namely, the program of studies and extracurriculum activities.

When this special study of Negro secondary schools was begun it was the plan to make only sufficient inquiry into the curriculum situation to identify the schools which would furnish rather complete data on this question, then to follow up the study in these with a more detailed curriculum investigation. Some of the problems contemplated for study in schools having more than one curriculum were: The year in which curriculums were first offered; the grade in which specialization for each curriculum is first allowed; the minimum and maximum number of units prescribed in each curriculum; and graduation requirements.

Because of the limited time and tardiness of responses to the first inquiry this follow-up study was abandoned. In consequence, the data finally obtained do not reveal as complete a picture regarding the offerings of high schools for colored children as might be desired.

2. TYPES OF CURRICULUMS

Principals of schools having one curriculum only were asked to designate whether it was academic, general, vocational, or some other. Table 15 reports a compilation of the replies to this question by size and type of school. Three hundred and forty schools responded. There seem to be no significant variations among the different size groups. One important feature of this table worthy of note, however, is the preponderance of schools indicating that the type of curriculum in their schools was vocational. This claim is not borne out by the subject offerings, which will be discussed later in this chapter, nor by the enrollments of pupils in the various curriculums, which will be discussed in Chapter VI.

Another feature of this table which defies explanation is the ratio between regular and reorganized schools, the curriculums of which are academic and vocational. Ordinarily reorganized schools are thought of as attempts to get away from the conventional, academic curriculum, and to offer an enriched curriculum. However, this table reveals that 41.3 per cent of the reorganized schools have academic curriculums as against only 27.5 per cent of the regular schools. Conversely, 66.7 per cent of the regular schools report vocational curriculums, while this is true of only 48 per cent of the reorganized schools. Both types of schools show very small percentages having general curriculums. One would not expect to find this situation obtaining among the reorganized schools. The type of response seems to indicate some misunderstanding of terms and the issues involved.

TABLE 15.—*Numbers and percentages of schools reporting certain types of curriculums, by size and type of school (Survey group)*

Curriculum	Size groups						Types		Total
	I	II	III	IV	V	VI	Regular	Reorganized	
1	2	3	4	5	6	7	8	9	10
Academic:									
Number	33	21	27	17	2	4	73	31	104
Per cent	29.7	32.8	31.3	42.5	12.5	17.3	27.5	41.3	30.5
Vocational:									
Number	67	42	53	21	13	17	177	36	213
Per cent	60.3	65.6	61.6	52.5	81.2	73.9	66.7	48.0	62.6
General:									
Number	9	1	6	1	------	2	12	7	19
Per cent	8.1	1.5	6.9	2.5	------	8.6	4.5	9.3	5.5
Other:									
Number	2	------	------	1	1	------	3	1	4
Per cent	1.8	------	------	2.5	6.2	------	1.1	1.3	1.1
Total schools replying	111	64	86	40	16	23	265	75	340

3. REQUIRED AND ELECTIVE OFFERINGS

The required and elective offerings in the various subject-matter fields by years for the entire group of Survey schools are shown in Table 16. It will be observed that English

TABLE 16.—*Numbers and percentages of schools offering required and elective courses in various subject-matter fields in each high-school year (Survey schools)*

Subject-matter fields	Year																	Rank as required subject	Rank as elective subject
	First				Second				Third				Fourth					
	Required		Elective		Required		Elective		Required		Elective		Required		Elective			
	Num-ber	Per cent	Num-ber	Per cent	Num-ber	Per cent	Num-ber	Per cent	Num-ber	Per cent	Num-ber	Per cent	Num-ber	Per cent	Num-ber	Per cent		
1	2	3	4	5	6	7	8	9	10	11	12	13	14	15	16	17	18	19
English	291	100	3	1.03	278	95.5	4	1.37	239	82.1	5	1.71	209	71.8	7	2.4	1	12
Mathematics	279	95.8	12	4.1	238	81.7	28	9.6	168	57.7	47	16.15	73	25.08	58	19.9	2	5
Science	180	61.8	49	16.8	156	53.6	55	18.9	111	38.1	70	24.05	104	35.7	75	25.7	4	3
Social science	193	66.0	45	15.4	191	65.6	56	19.2	160	54.9	50	17.1	173	59.4	42	14.4	3	4
Foreign language	77	26.4	71	24.3	76	26.1	88	30.2	77	26.4	123	42.2	69	23.7	114	39.1	5.5	1
Household and industrial arts	105	36.0	72	24.7	94	32.3	76	26.1	43	14.7	56	19.2	26	8.9	45	15.4	5.5	2
Commerce	3	1.0	9	3.0	5	1.7	13	4.4	4	1.3	19	6.5	6	2.0	19	6.5	11	8
Agriculture	31	10.6	24	8.2	28	9.6	21	7.2	10	3.4	19	6.5	6	2.0	15	5.1	9	7
Music	23	7.9	22	7.5	16	5.49	23	7.9	15	5.1	17	5.8	14	4.8	18	6.1	10	6
Fine arts	1	.3	8	2.7	1	.3	7	2.4	2	.6	4	1.3	2	.7	5	1.7	12	11
Health and physical education	34	11.6	9	3.0	27	9.2	8	2.7	24	8.2	8	2.7	21	7.2	8	2.7	7	9
Education and others	4	1.3	4	1.3	4	1.3	3	1.0	7	2.4	6	2.0	18	6.1	11	3.7	8	10

[41]

ranks first as a required subject, but holds twelfth place as an elective. The fact that foreign language holds first place as an elective and fifth as a required subject is a probable indication that it still has a strong hold on the schools, although evidence will be produced later in this chapter to show that it is losing ground.

In mathematics and science there is observed a definite tendency for the percentage of schools requiring them to decrease from year to year, and for the percentage of schools offering elective work in these subjects to increase. While this tendency may also be observed in social science and foreign language, it is not so consistent as in the two other subjects just mentioned. Another pronounced and consistent tendency may be observed in proceeding from the first year to the fourth in agriculture. In both cases of schools offering required and elective work in this subject the percentages move downward.

Some idea of the paucity of offerings in Negro high schools is evidenced in the small percentage of schools which offer even a small amount of work in commerce, music, and fine arts.

4. OFFERINGS BY SIZE OF SCHOOL

The percentages of schools offering required and elective work in the various subject-matter fields according to size groups are seen in Table 17. It will be observed that the amount of elective work increases and that of required work decreases proceeding from the first to the fourth year. Also the same general tendency is observed in proceeding from the smaller-sized schools to the larger ones within each year. There is a significant difference in favor of the larger schools in the richness of offerings as represented by the increase in percentages of schools offering electives.

The meagerness of offerings in some of the specialized subjects such as commerce, fine arts, and physical education and health is particularly to be noted.

TABLE 17.—*Percentages of schools offering required and elective courses in various subject fields in each high-school year according to size of school (statistical group)*

Subject field	First year						Second year						Third year						Fourth year					
	A	B	C	D	E	F	A	B	C	D	E	F	A	B	C	D	E	F	A	B	C	D	E	F
1	2	3	4	5	6	7	8	9	10	11	12	13	14	15	16	17	18	19	20	21	22	23	24	25
English:																								
Required	100	100	100	100	100	100	90	100	100	100	87	86	55	91	100	97	87	81	37	82	89	93	87	81
Elective	3.4	---	---	---	---	---	3.4	---	1.3	---	---	---	2.3	---	---	3.3	---	9.5	---	3	2.7	3.3	---	9.5
Mathematics:																								
Required	99	97	97	100	93	71	87	94	79	87	80	24	43	71	66	63	87	19	19	27	30	37	27	10
Elective	2.3	1.5	4.1	---	---	29	2.3	1.5	9.5	10	13	62	3.4	15	19	20	20	52	1.1	17	29	23	40	57
Science:																								
Required	59	71	63	67	73	24	51	70	62	43	33	14	24	47	51	43	40	14	15	53	51	40	33	9.5
Elective	10	4.5	12	20	27	76	9.3	7.5	19	33	27	67	5.8	17	29	40	47	67	4.6	17	27	63	60	57
Social studies:																								
Required	65	67	74	57	73	52	71	76	66	67	53	19	42	58	75	57	47	33	26	68	81	83	53	62
Elective	13	12	11	20	27	38	7	14	21	30	27	62	2.3	17	18	30	27	52	1.1	18	11	20	33	48
Foreign language:																								
Required	27	23	15	33	33	14	28	21	26	30	47	14	13	42	34	30	27	100	7	39	30	37	93	19
Elective	8.1	15	29	23	53	86	9.3	24	37	33	73	76	10	36	52	57	87	---	7	35	49	50	---	95
Household and industrial arts:																								
Required	35	35	37	43	33	33	23	31	37	40	33	43	9	14	16	20	27	19	3	8	12	20	13	5
Elective	15	21	30	13	53	52	15	21	33	27	53	43	3.4	17	23	33	40	43	4.6	12	16	30	47	24
Commerce:																								
Required	1	2	1	---	---	---	2	---	3	---	---	5	2	---	1	---	---	5	1	2	1	3	---	10
Elective	---	---	4.1	---	6.6	24	3.4	1.5	2.7	6.6	13	14	1.1	1.5	4.1	17	33	19	3.4	---	2.7	17	27	24
Agriculture:																								
Required	15	12	12	3	---	---	12	12	11	3	---	5	2	8	4	13	---	---	---	5	3	10	---	---
Elective	9.3	9	9.5	6.6	---	4.7	8.1	7.5	6.8	10	6.6	---	4.6	6	8.1	---	6.6	6.6	3.4	6	5.4	---	6.6	---

[43]

TABLE 17.—*Percentages of schools offering required and elective courses in various subject fields in each high-school year according to size of school (statistical group)*—Continued

Subject field	First year						Second year						Third year						Fourth year					
1	A 2	B 3	C 4	D 5	E 6	F 7	A 8	B 9	C 10	D 11	E 12	F 13	A 14	B 15	C 16	D 17	E 18	F 19	A 20	B 21	C 22	D 23	E 24	F 25
Music:																								
Required	5	6	7	10	7	29	5	2	7	7	13	10	6	2	5	7	13	5	3	3	7	3	13	5
Elective	1.1	7.5	9.5	13	13	14	1.1	9	6.8	10	20	24	--	6	4.1	13	13	19	--	7.5	5.4	10	13	19
Fine arts:																								
Required	--	--	--	--	--	5	--	--	--	--	--	5	--	--	--	--	--	10	--	--	3	--	--	--
Elective	2.3	1.5	2.7	--	--	24	2.3	--	--	--	6.6	19	--	--	1.3	--	--	14	--	--	1.3	6.6	--	9.5
Health and physical education:																								
Required	1	8	18	7	20	48	1	3	18	10	7	33	--	8	12	7	7	33	1	3	12	7	7	29
Elective	1.1	4.5	1.3	10	--	4.7	1.1	7.5	1.3	3.3	--	--	--	6	1.3	10	--	--	2.3	6	--	6.6	--	--
Education and related subjects:																								
Required	--	2	3	--	7	--	1	--	3	--	7	--	2	--	4	--	13	--	5	2	12	3	20	--
Elective	--	1.5	4.1	--	--	--	--	1.5	2.7	--	--	--	1.1	1.5	2.7	3.3	6.6	--	2.3	3	4.1	10	6.6	--

NOTE.—Read table thus: English is required in the first year by 100 per cent of the schools in all size groups and it is an elective subject in 3.4 per cent of the schools in Group A, in the first year. Mathematics is required in the first year by 99 percent of the schools in Group A, 97 per cent in Group B, and so on. It is an elective subject in 2.3 per cent of the schools in Group A and 1.5 per cent in Group B.

5. CURRICULUM TRENDS

In order to ascertain the trends in the programs of studies in Negro high schools, principals were requested to list the courses added to and dropped from their offerings during the past five years (1925–1930). The results of this investigation are reported in Table 18. Two hundred and ninety-one schools gave responses sufficiently clear and accurate to be included in the study. These schools added 209 courses and dropped 119. The average number of courses added per school is 2, and the average number dropped per school is 1.6. This latter figure is in close correspondence with the average number of courses dropped per school by the 4-year unselected white high schools represented in Monograph No. 6 of this Survey on the smaller secondary schools, their average being 1.5. There is a greater difference, however, between the two groups of schools in the average number of courses added to the program of studies within the past five years. The average for the white group is 3.6 as compared with 2 for the colored group.

The average number of courses introduced per school into the program of studies by the white and colored schools by size groups is as follows:

	I	II	III	IV	V	VI	Total
White	2. 8	3. 6	3. 7	3. 5	4. 1	_ _ _	3. 6
Colored	1. 8	1. 8	1. 5	3. 7	2. 1	2. 7	2. 0

Group V for the white schools corresponds to V and VI for the colored schools. The comparative figures for the average number of courses dropped per school are:

	I	II	III	IV	V	VI	Total
White	1. 0	1. 7	1. 3	1. 3	1. 8	_ _ _	1. 5
Colored	2. 7	1. 2	1. 5	1. 0	1. 3	1. 0	1. 6

The following important fact is shown in Table 18: The contrast between the average number of courses added per school by the three smallest groups with the same items for the three groups of largest schools gives the latter a distinct advantage. The converse is true, however, with reference to the courses dropped. In this case the small groups have the largest average per school.

TABLE 18.—*Number of courses in the various subject fields which were added and dropped during the past five years by a given number of schools of varying sizes (Survey schools)*

A. COURSES ADDED

Group of schools	Number schools in group	Courses added and dropped	English	Mathematics	Science	Social studies	Foreign language	Household and industrial arts	Commerce	Agriculture	Music	Fine arts	Health and physical education	Education and related subjects	Average per school
1	2	3	4	5	6	7	8	9	10	11	12	13	14	15	16
I	86	42	2	6	15	23	5	14	0	7	4	0	2	4	1.9
II	66	58	3	9	29	18	11	17	2	7	2	1	3	3	1.8
III	73	64	2	6	24	23	14	12	4	4	4	0	3	4	1.5
IV	30	18	3	6	14	9	8	4	17	2	0	0	1	4	3.7
V	15	11	0	2	4	4	4	2	5	1	0	0	0	1	2.1
VI	21	16	4	1	4	6	7	10	7	0	2	0	3	0	2.7
Total	291	209	14	30	90	83	49	59	35	21	12	1	12	16	2.0

B. COURSES DROPPED

Group of schools	Number schools in group	Courses added and dropped	English	Mathematics	Science	Social studies	Foreign language	Household and industrial arts	Commerce	Agriculture	Music	Fine arts	Health and physical education	Education and related subjects	Average per school
I	86	29	0	5	11	3	25	30	2	0	0	0	2	1	2.7
II	66	32	0	1	7	6	14	5	0	2	0	0	1	2	1.2
III	73	40	0	7	7	5	23	1	5	4	0	0	1	5	1.5
IV	30	9	0	1	2	5	0	1	0	0	0	0	0	0	1.0
V	15	3	0	1	2	0	1	0	0	0	0	0	0	0	1.3
VI	21	6	0	0	0	0	1	0	2	0	0	0	3	0	1.0
Total	291	119	0	14	28	16	69	36	10	6	0	0	7	8	1.6

On the basis of these data it appears that the small schools are making an effort to simplify their programs of studies. Accurate comparisons can not be made between the size groups for the individual subject fields because the number of schools varies. However, comparisons can be made between courses dropped and courses added within a given field. Viewing the table from this standpoint, the following facts are evident: First, in every subject, except one, the number of courses added exceeds the number dropped; second, the excess number of courses added over those dropped in science and social studies is very pronounced; third, foreign language suffers in this comparison, the courses dropped exceeding those added by 20. Of the 69 foreign language courses which were dropped, 54 were Latin, 11 were French, 2 were German, and 2 were Greek. Of the 48 courses in foreign language added during the past five years, 12 were Latin, 26 were French, 7 were Spanish, 1 was German, 1 was general language, 1 was modern language. Of the 83 courses in social science which were added, 18 were courses in Negro history.

Of the 80 courses in science which were added, the 5 courses having the highest frequence of mention were: Chemistry, 25; biology, 19; physics, 17; geography, 12; and general science, 8. Of the 28 courses in science which were dropped, the courses having the highest frequency of mention were: Chemistry, 6; geography, 6; biology, 5; physics, 5; and general science, 4.

6. THE EXTRACURRICULUM

No phase of secondary-school work has gained in popularity more rapidly in recent years than extracurriculum activities. They are taking an important place in the life of the school as socializing and integrating agencies. Table 19 presents the facts relating to this part of the Survey of Negro secondary schools. There is a constant increase in the percentage of schools fostering certain types of activities as the size of school increases. This tendency is pronounced in the following activities: Dramatic club, school paper, school annual, orchestra, band, science club, language club, student government organization, and football.

Other facts of interest are the type and rankings of the first 12 activities which were fostered by the largest percentages of the schools. Table 20 shows these activities ranked according to the percentage of schools fostering them. Six of these activities are athletic in nature; one is musical; two literary; and one artistic. This table also shows the percentage of white schools fostering these activities. The percentages for the athletic activities fostered by white schools were taken from the study of smaller high schools reported in Monograph No. 6 of this Survey. The activities mentioned were among the highest 12. The fact that the percentages for the white schools are in most cases smaller than for the colored schools probably is a reflection of the larger variety of possible activities from which white pupils may select.

TABLE 19.—*Number and percentages of schools fostering certain types of extracurriculum activities*

Activity	Size groups												Total	
	I		II		III		IV		V		VI			
	Number	Per cent	Number	Per cent	Number	Per cent	Number	Per cent	Number	Per cent	Number	Per cent	Number	Per cent
1	2	3	4	5	6	7	8	9	10	11	12	13	14	15
Literary clubs	85	67.4	51	59.3	68	67.3	36	83.7	16	94.0	26	76.4	282	69.2
Debating clubs	38	30.1	33	38.3	52	51.4	30	69.7	12	70.5	21	61.7	186	45.7
Dramatic clubs	32	25.3	31	36.0	51	50.4	31	72.0	12	70.5	31	91.1	188	46.1
Glee clubs	87	69.0	70	81.4	80	79.2	36	83.7	15	88.2	30	88.2	318	78.1
School paper	13	10.3	12	13.9	29	28.7	20	46.5	8	47.0	29	85.2	111	27.2
School annual	1	.7	2	2.0	9	8.9	3	6.9	3	17.6	14	41.1	32	7.8
Orchestra	17	13.4	9	10.4	17	16.8	11	25.5	9	52.9	22	64.7	85	20.8
Band	9	7.1	6	6.9	13	12.8	8	18.6	5	29.4	12	35.2	53	13.0
4-H clubs	16	12.6	12	13.9	13	13.8	5	11.6	2	11.7	4	11.7	52	12.8
Agriculture clubs	39	29.3	24	27.9	22	21.7	11	25.5	5	29.4	3	8.8	103	25.0
Science clubs	11	8.7	14	16.2	29	28.7	22	51.1	8	47.0	26	76.4	110	27.0
Language clubs	22	17.4	15	17.4	22	21.7	15	34.8	7	41.1	26	76.4	107	26.2
Student-government organizations	11	8.7	16	18.6	20	19.8	10	23.2	7	41.1	23	67.6	87	21.3
Football	41	32.5	40	46.5	65	64.3	33	76.7	13	76.4	29	85.2	221	54.2
Baseball	93	73.8	71	82.5	73	72.2	31	72.0	11	64.7	28	82.3	307	75.9
Track	32	25.3	17	19.7	40	38.6	17	39.5	5	29.4	24	73.5	135	33.1
Tennis	32	25.3	38	44.1	46	45.5	13	30.2	7	41.1	17	50.0	153	37.5
Basket ball	98	77.7	81	94.1	88	87.1	36	83.7	16	94.0	34	100.0	353	86.7
Volley ball	37	29.3	24	27.9	33	32.6	15	34.8	8	47.0	17	50.0	134	32.2
Handball	15	11.9	6	6.9	16	15.8	4	9.3	2	11.7	7	20.5	50	12.2
Indoor baseball	9	7.1	5	5.8	8	7.9	7	16.2	3	17.6	13	38.2	45	11.0
Hockey	1	.7			3	2.9	1	2.3			2	5.2	7	1.7
Soccer	2	1.5	3	3.4	2	1.0			2	11.7	8	23.5	17	4.1
Others	29	23.0	27	31.4	55	54.4	30	69.7	6	35.2	45		192	47.1
Average number of activities per school	6.0		7.0		8.4		9.8		10.7		14.4		8.1	

TABLE 20.—*Twelve extracurriculum activities ranked according to the percentage of Negro schools fostering them and the percentage of white schools fostering the same activities*

Activity	Percentage of schools		Activity	Percentage of schools	
	Negro	White [1]		Negro	White [1]
Basket ball	86.7	94.8	Debating club	45.7	38.4
Glee club	78.1	74.3	Tennis	37.5	43.5
Baseball	75.4	63.0	Track	33.1	63.8
Literary club	69.2	29.5	Volley ball	32.2	34.1
Football	54.2	57.6	School paper	27.2	55.5
Dramatic club	46.1	53.9	Science club	27.0	18.6

[1] Data are from Monograph No. 6. Op. cit.

As shown in Table 19 the contrast between the different groups in the average number of activities fostered per school is of particular importance; the minimum is 6 for Group I, and the maximum is 14.4 for Group VI. This shows the advantage the larger schools have in the matter of providing extracurriculum activities.

7. SUMMARY

According to evidence presented here, it is found that some uncertainty exists with reference to the meaning of the various curriculums in Negro schools. Although the total number of courses added to the programs of studies during the past five years exceeds the number dropped, the paucity of offering is still pronounced, especially in commerce, music, and art. The larger schools far surpass the smaller ones in the richness and variety of their offerings, both in regular school subjects and in extracurriculum activities, and the white schools are superior to the colored schools in richness of curriculum and extracurriculum offerings.

The concerns of the chapter.—How are colored children availing themselves of the secondary-school facilities which are offered them? In what courses of study do they enroll most extensively? What is the holding power of the Negro high schools? To what extent do they stimulate a continuing interest in education? And what differences are there between Negro boys and girls in reference to these factors? This chapter is concerned with finding answers to these questions.

The facts on enrollment.—High school enrollment of a people is not only influenced by their economic status, but also by their social and intellectual development and their general cultural level. Enrollment of colored pupils in high schools is perhaps one of the best criteria by which to measure the general progress of the race since emancipation. The popularization of secondary education among them has been a subject of favorable comment by everyone who has studied the question. The extent of this popularizing process may be seen by reference to Figure 7.

Here are shown the trends in high-school enrollment for white and colored pupils since 1892. The rate of increase for whites was greater than that for colored during the first two periods from 1892 to 1910; but beginning with 1920 and for each biennial period thereafter the rate of increase of colored enrollment was far in excess of that for whites. Particular attention is directed to the rapid upturn of the curve for Negroes from 1922 to 1930.

The enrollment of colored and white pupils in secondary schools and the percentage of increase in the enrollments for specified periods are shown in Table 21. It is of particular significance to note that the percentage of increase of the enrollment of Negro pupils in 1930 over 1920 was 506.2 as compared with 175.7 for white pupils over the same period. This disproportion of increase in high-school enrollment be-

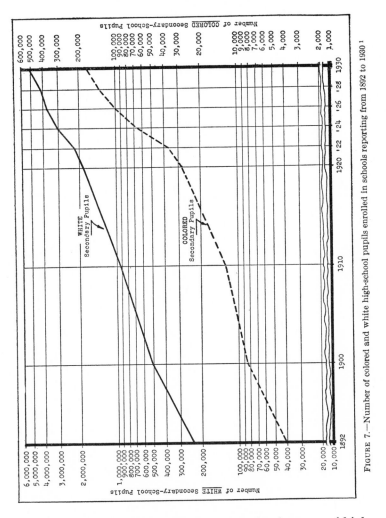

FIGURE 7.—Number of colored and white high-school pupils enrolled in schools reporting from 1892 to 1930 [1]

tween the two races is a reflection of the inadequacy of high-school provisions for Negroes prior to 1920.

[1] The data were secured from the Biennial Survey reports of the Office of Education, enrollment figures of 1892 being used instead of those of 1890, because they seemed to be more nearly accurate. It should be noted that enrollment figures for colored pupils are found in the extreme left column.

TABLE 21.—*Enrollments of colored and white pupils in secondary schools and percentage of increase in enrollment by specified periods* [1]

Race	1892	1900	1910	1920	1922
1	2	3	4	5	6
Colored:					
Enrollment	4,047	8,395	12,636	27,631	35,731
Percentage of increase each enrollment is over the next preceding		107.4	50.5	118.6	29.3
White:					
Enrollment	235,509	510,856	902,425	1,829,524	2,193,676
Percentage of increase each enrollment is over the next preceding		116.9	76.6	102.7	19.9

Race	1924	1926	1928	1930
1	7	8	9	10
Colored:				
Enrollment	63,405	98,705	132,329	167,515
Percentage of increase each enrollment is over the next preceding	77.4	55.6	34	26.5
White:				
Enrollment	2,950,408	3,642,368	4,084,984	5,044,664
Percentage of increase each enrollment is of the next preceding	34.4	23.4	12.1	[2] 23.4

[1] Report of the U. S. Commissioner of Education.
[2] Per cent of increase from 1920 to 1930 is: Colored, 506.2; white, 175.7.

2. ATTENDANCE

From a cursory view of several bodies of data there appeared to be slight differences between white and colored pupils in the matter of attendance in high school; consequently, investigation of this item was not continued. An effort was made, however, to ascertain the causes of poor attendance where it existed. Principals were asked to name the factors which they considered of first importance in causing poor attendance. The results of this study are shown in Table 22. "Work" assumes a high rank as a cause of poor attendance, leading in each group of schools except those in Group VI, the large city schools, where "poverty" is cited by 30 per cent of the principals as against 26.6 per cent for "work." Those factors over which the pupil has control or to which he can readily adapt himself have a small percentage of citations.

TABLE 22.—*Percentages of principals naming factors considered of first importance in causing poor attendance, according to size of schools (Survey schools)*

Size groups	Factors named									
	Work	Weather	Distance	Poverty	Illness	Parental indifference	Training	Out of town	Other	Total schools replying
1	2	3	4	5	6	7	8	9	10	11
I	52.0	5.2	5.2	11.4	6.2	16.6	2.0		1.0	96
II	63.9		8.2	13.1	3.2	11.4				61
III	52.9	3.5	4.7	8.2	16.4	14.1				85
IV	48.4	3.0		30.3	9.0	9.0				33
V	41.6			33.3	8.3	8.3	8.3			12
VI	26.6	3.3		30.0	23.3	13.3			3.3	30
Total schools replying	163	10	14	49	33	43	3		2	317
Per cent of total schools replying	51.4	3.1	4.4	15.4	10.4	13.5	.9		.6	100

3. CURRICULUM REGISTRATION

The enrollment of white and colored pupils in the various curriculums by type and size of school is shown in Table 23. These data were obtained from the schools designated above as statistical schools. The study according to type of school and size group includes 99,093 colored pupils and 1,160,542 white pupils. These numbers appear to be sufficiently large, other things being equal, to make valid whatever conclusions may be reached regarding the drawing power of the various curriculums, or the tendency in the matter of required curriculum offerings.

The facts revealed in this table do not tend to substantiate the evidence for the Survey schools, discussed in Chapter V, namely, that of the schools having only one curriculum in 62.6 per cent of the cases it was the vocational curriculum. In order to obtain further light on this question, a study was made of the 220 schools belonging to the Survey group which were also included in the statistical group with respect to the curriculum registration of their pupils. The results of this study conformed rather closely to the general results shown in Table 15. Of the 46,913 pupils enrolled in these 220 schools, 44 per cent are registered in general, 40 per cent in academic,

TABLE 23.—*Percentages of white and colored pupils enrolled in the various curriculums by type and size of "statistical" schools (W, white; C, colored)*

Group	Academic (classical and scientific)		General		Commercial		Manual training		Training course for teachers		Agriculture		Home economics		Industrial or trade		Enrollment	
	W	C	W	C	W	C	W	C	W	C	W	C	W	C	W	C	W	C
1	2	3	4	5	6	7	8	9	10	11	12	13	14	15	16	17	18	19
Type:																		
Reorganized	44.0	45.4	45.0	44.5	5.7	2.5	1.6	2.7	0.09	0.1	0.6	0.3	1.8	3.7	0.7	0.5	468,325	40,695
Regular	44.9	42.2	46.0	50.1	4.8	1.0	1.3	2.5	.05	0	.9	.3	1.5	2.6	.2	.9	692,217	58,398
Size:																		
I	47.0	39.6	52.6	58.4	.1	0	0	0	0	0	.1	.7	.3	1.1	0	0	76,214	8,281
II	46.7	43.5	52.2	55.3	.3	0	.008	0	.03	0	.2	.3	.4	.7	0	0	89,087	5,631
III	49.4	44.5	45.8	51.5	1.5	.04	.07	.3	.1	.08	1.4	.7	1.4	2.1	.006	.5	349,661	23,508
IV	45.7	41.2	44.5	52.7	3.6	2.8	.3	.2	.05	0	1.8	1.1	2.6	1.7	.9	0	127,931	9,259
V	45.0	47.5	45.4	50.1	5.3	.7	.7	.5	.03	.2	1.0	0	2.1	1.7	.1	0	141,167	10,893
VI	38.4	43.2	43.0	40.9	11.1	3.0	4.0	5.9	.03	0	.1	0	2.0	5.2	.9	1.5	376,482	41,521
Total	44.5	43.5	45.6	47.8	5.1	1.6	1.4	2.6	.07	.04	.8	.3	1.6	3.0	.4	.7	1,160,542	99,093

and 15 per cent in vocational curriculums. The lack of agreement between curriculum claims on the part of schools and curriculum registrations of pupils is probably due to a difference in definition of the types of curriculums, a confusion already mentioned.

With regard to the reorganized and regular schools a similar situation is found concerning registration of white pupils in academic curriculums as obtained in the Survey schools. In the case of colored pupils more registered in academic curriculums in the reorganized schools than in the regular schools. The registrations in academic curriculums in the two types of schools are practically the same in terms of percentages of the total registrants.

It is of interest to note that a larger percentage of pupils of both races are registered in general curriculums in the regular schools than in the reorganized schools. In view of the avowed objectives of the reorganized schools the converse would be expected.

Considering the total group, there are only slight differences between the registrations of colored and white pupils in the academic and general curriculums. There is a decided difference, however, between the two groups in percentages of pupils registering in commercial curriculums. One explanation of this that may be advanced is the fact that only a few schools for Negroes offer commercial work, as revealed in Chapter V, Table 17.

There appear to be no significant differences in registration in academic curriculums by schools according to size groups; but in general curriculums the percentage of pupils registered decreases as the size of school increases. This probably may be explained by the fact that general curriculums are offered by a greater number of small schools, located in rural and village communities, than is true of the larger schools.

As is to be expected, the percentage of pupils registering in commercial curriculums show a distinct trend upward as the size of school increases.

4. HOLDING POWER OF THE SCHOOLS

One index of educational efficiency frequently applied to school systems and individual schools is the percentage of their pupils who remain to graduate. Tables 24, 25, and 26 present facts regarding this item according to States, size, and type of schools. Data for these tables were obtained from the 688 schools of the statistical group, enrolling 105,406 pupils. For the 18 States studied, there were 9,105 graduates, or 8.6 per cent of the total enrollment. In Table 24 it may be observed that the percentages of male graduates to the total male enrollment in the various States range from 4.4 to 10. The range for the female graduates is 5.5 to 11.3 per cent.

TABLE 24.—*Negro high-school enrollment, numbers of graduates, and percentages graduates are of high-school enrollment, 1930 (statistical schools)*

State	Enroll-ment	Graduates					
		Boys		Girls		Total	
		Num-ber	Per cent	Num-ber	Per cent	Num-ber	Per cent
1	2	3	4	5	6	7	8
Alabama	6,885	210	8.6	423	9.5	633	9.1
Arkansas	2,455	54	5.9	91	5.8	145	5.9
Delaware	741	27	7.9	35	8.7	62	8.3
District of Columbia	6,576	164	6.1	235	6.0	399	5.1
Florida	3,095	57	5.4	142	6.9	199	6.4
Georgia	5,812	156	8.1	269	6.9	425	7.3
Kentucky	3,493	133	10.0	239	11.0	372	10.6
Louisiana	2,705	71	8.1	168	9.1	239	8.8
Maryland	6,330	148	6.0	311	7.9	459	7.0
Mississippi	3,172	44	4.4	121	5.5	165	5.2
Missouri	6,457	187	6.7	375	10.1	562	8.7
North Carolina	14,384	469	9.5	1,078	11.3	1,547	10.7
Oklahoma	4,547	167	8.9	287	10.7	454	9.9
South Carolina	3,847	106	9.0	272	10.1	378	9.8
Tennessee	6,919	227	9.6	511	11.1	738	10.6
Texas	15,096	534	9.2	1,005	10.8	1,539	10.1
Virginia	6,239	164	7.2	369	9.2	533	8.5
West Virginia	3,490	95	6.4	161	8.0	256	7.3
Total	105,406	3,013	7.7	6,092	9.1	9,105	8.6

A comparison of white and colored pupils in percentages the graduates are of the enrollment according to size group is afforded in Table 25. One feature of special importance about these data which is not shown in the table is the ratio between the percentage the enrollment in each size group is of the total enrollment and the percentage the graduates in these groups are of the total number of graduates. For whites the percentage the enrollment in Group A is of the total is 5.9, and the percentage the graduates are of the total graduates is 4. The corresponding percentages for Negroes are 7.8 and 3.7. In Group B for whites the enrollment percentage is 6.9, for graduates, 7.6; for Negroes they are 5.3 and 5.3. Groups D and E present similar ratios; but in Groups C and F there is a decided contrast. The enrollment percentages for whites in Groups C and F are 27.2 and 37, respectively, a difference of 10, yet the percentages their graduates are of the total graduates are 32.3 for Group C, and 32.1 for Group F. There is some unexplained factor operating to give Group C a larger percentage, and Group F a smaller percentage of the white graduates than their enrollment percentages seem to warrant.

TABLE 25.—*Numbers of colored and white pupils enrolled in high schools in 1930, and number and percentage the 1930 graduates are of the enrollment, by size of school (statistical schools)*

Groups of pupils	Size groups of schools						Total
	A	B	C	D	E	F	
1	2	3	4	5	6	7	8
BOYS Enrollment:							
White	35,053	40,170	160,691	61,267	76,231	229,820	603,232
Colored	3,070	2,012	8,776	3,373	3,880	17,819	38,930
Graduates:							
White	2,500	4,593	19,883	4,237	7,560	20,763	62,536
Colored	124	168	849	255	306	1,311	3,013
Per cent graduates are of enrollment:							
White	7.5	12.2	13.7	14.3	13.3	12.6	12.8
Colored	4.3	9.2	11.4	11.0	10.6	9.9	9.9
GIRLS Enrollment:							
White	41,092	49,032	190,267	70,240	85,808	245,998	682,437
Colored	5,207	3,667	14,634	5,998	7,282	29,688	66,476
Graduates:							
White	3,469	6,664	27,905	9,951	10,502	26,793	85,284
Colored	219	319	1,717	502	698	2,637	6,092
Per cent graduates are of enrollment:							
White	8.8	14.4	16.1	16.9	16.0	15.0	15.2
Colored	4.4	9.6	13.3	11.7	14.7	11.7	11.3
TOTAL Enrollment:							
White	76,145	89,202	350,958	131,507	162,039	475,818	1,285,669
Colored	8,277	5,679	23,410	9,371	11,162	47,507	105,406
Graduates:							
White	5,969	11,257	47,788	17,188	18,062	47,556	147,820
Colored	343	487	2,566	757	1,007	3,948	9,105
Per cent graduates are of enrollment:							
White	8.2	13.4	15.0	15.7	14.7	13.9	14.1
Colored	4.4	9.4	12.6	11.5	11.6	11.1	10.8

The colored schools also present some interesting facts in these two groups. In Group C the colored graduates constitute a larger percentage of the total graduates than the percentage of the enrollment in that group is of the total enrollment, the percentages being for enrollment and graduates, respectively, 22.2 and 28.1.

TABLE 26.—*Number and percentage of colored pupils enrolled in high school in 1930, and number and percentage the 1930 graduates are of the enrollment, by type of school (statistical schools)*

Item	Senior high schools	Junior-senior high schools	Undivided 5-year high schools	Undivided 6-year high schools	All reorganized schools	Regular 4-year high schools	Total
1	2	3	4	5	6	7	8
Enrollment	2,357	18,098	617	11,251	32,323	52,953	85,276
Per cent of total	2.2	17.1	.5	10.6	37.7	50.2	
Graduates	169	1,543	61	836	2,609	6,496	9,105
Per cent graduates are of enrollment	7.1	8.5	9.8	7.4	7.7	12.2	10.6
Per cent of all graduates	1.8	16.9	.6	9.1	28.4	71.3	100

In Group F there is a slight difference in favor of the enrollment percentage. From the facts presented it can be seen that Group C has a decidedly stronger holding power for both races in the schools studied here than schools in other size groups. Another interesting fact brought out is that the large schools, as represented by Group F, seem to lack the strength expected of them in holding their pupils until graduation, as shown by the percentage the graduates are of the enrollment. This is true for both races, but particularly for the whites. This situation is probably due to the multiplicity of interests and opportunity for work presented these students in the urban centers represented.

Facts concerning the holding power of various types of schools are revealed in Table 26. It will be observed that there are distinct differences between the schools in the percentages the graduates are of the enrollments. If the assumption is accepted that these percentages are an index of the holding power of a school, it can be said that the regular high schools are superior to other types of schools in this regard. The percentages the graduates are of enrollments for all types of schools are: Senior high schools, 7.1; junior high schools, 8.5; undivided 5-year high schools, 9.8; undivided 6-year high schools, 7.4; regular 4-year high schools 12.2. For all types of reorganized schools combined the percentage the graduates are of the enrollments is 7.7. Further study of this subject is required before any plausible explanation can be advanced concerning the differences between the various types of schools in their ability to hold pupils.

5. GRADUATES CONTINUING THEIR EDUCATION

By States.—The numbers and percentages of high-school graduates in 1929 who were reported as continuing their edu-

State	Entering College		Entering Other Institutions		Total Continuing Education		Grand Total Continuing Education		Per Cent Continuing Education
	Number	Per Cent	Number	Per Cent	Number	Per Cent	Number	Per Cent	
Alabama	5 / 17	1.9 / 4.1	6 / 29	4.7 / 7.0	11 / 46	8.7 / 11.2	57	10.6	
Arkansas	16 / 35	42.1 / 37.6	0 / 4	0.0 / 4.3	16 / 39	42.1 / 41.9	55	41.9	
Delaware	7 / 6	29.1 / 18.1	0 / 0	0.0 / 0.0	7 / 6	29.1 / 18.1	13	22.8	
District of Columbia	43 / 42	26.1 / 13.9	1 / 83	0.6 / 27.5	44 / 125	26.7 / 41.5	169	37.2	
Florida	56 / 105	75.6 / 68.6	0 / 10	0.0 / 6.5	56 / 115	75.6 / 75.1	171	75.3	
Georgia	21 / 20	47.7 / 23.2	8 / 18	18.1 / 20.9	29 / 38	45.9 / 44.1	67	51.5	
Kentucky	51 / 88	45.1 / 45.3	8 / 15	7.0 / 7.7	59 / 103	52.2 / 53.0	162	52.7	
Louisiana	18 / 30	51.4 / 20.4	1 / 1	2.8 / 0.6	19 / 31	54.2 / 21.0	50	27.4	
Maryland	41 / 38	28.0 / 14.5	25 / 49	17.1 / 18.7	66 / 87	45.2 / 33.2	153	37.5	
Mississippi	19 / 36	48.7 / 25.7	3 / 10	7.6 / 7.1	22 / 46	56.4 / 32.8	68	37.8	
Missouri	70 / 84	38.8 / 28.0	5 / 51	2.7 / 17.0	75 / 135	41.6 / 45.1	210	43.8	
North Carolina	142 / 273	47.3 / 40.1	14 / 130	4.6 / 19.1	156 / 403	52.0 / 59.2	559	57.0	
Oklahoma	25 / 39	51.0 / 46.9	3 / 7	6.1 / 8.4	28 / 46	57.1 / 55.4	74	56.0	
South Carolina	57 / 81	67.8 / 44.5	4 / 11	4.7 / 6.5	61 / 92	72.6 / 55.0	153	60.9	
Tennessee	87 / 133	44.8 / 41.4	2 / 14	1.0 / 4.3	89 / 147	45.8 / 45.7	236	45.8	
Texas	177 / 316	51.7 / 50.0	18 / 41	5.2 / 6.4	195 / 357	57.0 / 56.4	552	56.6	
Virginia	65 / 141	58.0 / 46.8	7 / 41	6.2 / 13.6	72 / 182	64.2 / 60.4	294	61.5	
West Virginia	49 / 89	51.5 / 55.6	4 / 3	4.2 / 1.8	53 / 92	55.7 / 57.5	145	56.8	
Total	949 / 1573	44.1 / 35.2	109 / 517	5.0 / 11.5	1058 / 2090	49.2 / 46.8	3148	47.6	

FIGURE 8.—Number and percentage of Negro high-school graduates of 1929, by sex, who were continuing their education in 1930 in 17 Southern States and the District of Columbia

cation in 1930 are given for 17 States and the District of Columbia in Figure 8. In the fourth column will be seen the total number of boys and girls combined who are continuing their education in college or some other institution, and the percentage this number is of the 1929 graduates for each State. The small percentage shown for Alabama is probably an error. It is believed that many principals in that State failed to answer this particular question. The other columns in the figure analyze the total situation found in Column 4.

By size of school.—A comparison by size of schools of the percentages of white and colored graduates who continue their education reveals no significant differences among the schools in the first five size groups for either race. In the sixth group, however, comprising schools enrolling 500 or more pupils, there is a decided drop in the percentages for both races. Again, the factor of varied avenues open to pupils in large cities is offered as the probable explanation of this drop in percentages of graduates continuing their education.

A more important fact, however, brought out by this comparison is the amount by which the percentage of colored graduates continuing their education exceeds the percentage of white graduates continuing in every group except those in the large cities. The following explanations are offered for this occurrence: First, the colored graduates are probably a more highly selected group, within their own race, than is true of the white graduates. The small percentage of Negro population of high-school age enrolled in high school, as shown in Chapter V; the small survival percentage as shown by the small percentage the high-school enrollment is of the total enrollment, pointed out in the same chapter; and the small percentage the colored graduates are of the high-school enrollment all tend to substantiate this theory. It has the further corroboration of the earlier high proportion of high-school graduates going on among whites when the high school was for the whites much more predominantly a college preparatory institution. Most Negro high schools are now at a stage of development formerly characteristic of schools for whites.

A second probable explanation is the fact that many of the opportunities not requiring further formal training which are open to white high-school graduates are closed to colored graduates. Negroes have found their greatest outlet for advancement in the professions, which require additional training beyond high school. Because of this factor, and because of the highly selective nature of the group, a larger percentage of the few colored pupils who have enrolled in high school and finally graduated, continue their education than of the large number of whites who enroll and graduate.

By sex.—In Figure 9 are shown, according to sex and by race, the facts about graduates who continue their education. It will be observed that the percentage of colored boys continuing their education exceeds the girls in all groups except two, while the percentage of white boys who continue is less than the white girls in every group except two. For all groups combined the percentage of colored boys continuing their education also exceeds the colored girls. In the case of the whites, however, the reverse is true.

The explanation offered for the fact that colored boys are ahead of the girls in this respect is similar to the one advanced concerning the percentage of colored and white graduates continuing their education. As will be shown later the actual number of colored boys in high school as compared with colored girls is very small. Likewise, the percentage that the colored male graduates is of the colored male enrollment is less than the corresponding percentage for colored girls. It, therefore, follows that the boys who do graduate are probably a highly selected group. Moreover, the avenues open to the boys who graduate from high school are probably less attractive than those offered colored girls. Furthermore, from personnel studies of Negro students,[1] it is shown that most of the boys contemplate a professional career, which necessitates additional training beyond high school.

6. RATIOS OF NEGRO BOYS AND GIRLS

One of the most insistent problems facing Negroes to-day is the great disparity in the proportions of boys and girls enrolled in school, the proportion of girls exceeding that of boys. This difference begins to show itself in the early grades and rises steadily until it reaches the fourth year in high school, and continues even into college. Figure 10 is a demonstration of the differences. It will be noted that the percentages

---

[1] Bullock, R. W. A Study of the Occupational Choices of Negro High-School Boys. Crisis, 37 : 301-303, September, 1930. Caliver, Ambrose. A Personnel Study of Negro College Students. Teachers College, Columbia University, New York City, 1931. (Teachers College Contributions to Education, No. 484.)

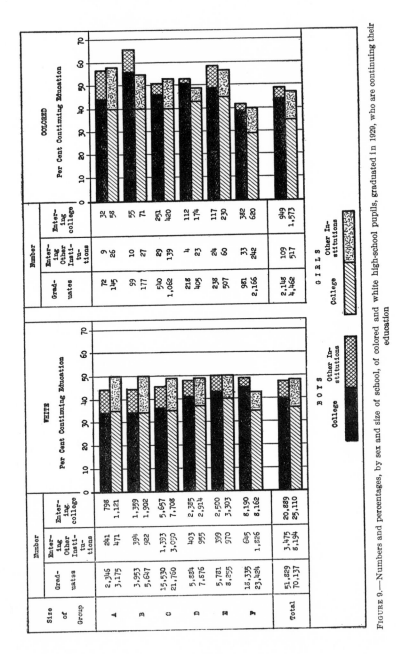

FIGURE 9.—Numbers and percentages, by sex and size of school, of colored and white high-school pupils, graduated in 1929, who are continuing their education

by which the enrollments of girls surpass those of boys have a range from 18.5 for Delaware to 127.6 for South Carolina. The data for this figure and the one next following were obtained from the 688 schools of the statistical group, enrolling 105,406 Negro high-school pupils.

State	Enrollment		Percentages by which the enrollments of girls surpass those of boys	Enrollment				
	Girls	Boys		0 2000 4000 6000 8000 10000				
Alabama	4,449	2,436	82.6					
Arkansas	1,554	901	72.4					
Delaware	402	339	18.5					
District of Columbia	3,909	2,667	46.5					
Florida	2,052	1,043	96.7					
Georgia	3,887	1,925	101.9					
Kansas	1,778	1,385	28.3					
Kentucky	2,171	1,322	64.2					
Louisiana	1,834	871	110.5					
Maryland	3,888	2,442	59.2					
Mississippi	2,180	992	119.7					
Missouri	3,702	2,755	34.3					
North Carolina	9,459	4,925	92.0					
Oklahoma	2,674	1,873	42.7					
South Carolina	2,673	1,174	127.6					
Tennessee	4,568	2,351	94.3					
Texas	9,297	5,799	60.3					
Virginia	3,989	2,250	77.2					
West Virginia	2,010	1,480	35.8					

Boys ▆ Girls ▆

FIGURE 10.—Enrollment of Negro boys and girls in high school and percentages by which enrollments of girls surpass those of boys, by States (statistical schools)

In Figure 11 are shown the ratio between boys and girls by high-school grades and types of schools. From a cursory examination of the data on ratios according to size of school there did not seem to be any significant differences among the size groups. An examination of the figure reveals a decided progressive increase of the percentage the enrollment of girls is greater than boys from the first year to the fourth year of high school. For all schools combined the percentages are: First year, 64.8; second year, 78.8; third year, 85.8; and fourth year, 90.6.

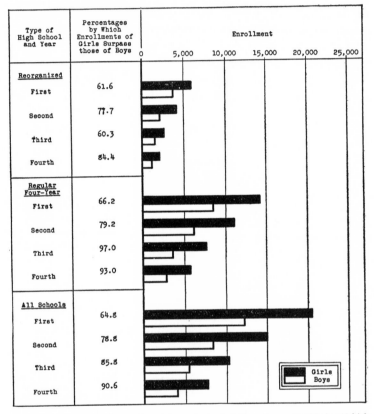

Type of High School and Year	Percentages by Which Enrollments of Girls Surpass those of Boys	Enrollment
Reorganized		
First	61.6	
Second	77.7	
Third	60.3	
Fourth	84.4	
Regular Four-Year		
First	66.2	
Second	79.2	
Third	97.0	
Fourth	93.0	
All Schools		
First	64.8	
Second	78.8	
Third	85.8	
Fourth	90.6	

FIGURE 11.—Enrollment by grade and type of school of Negro boys and girls in 688 high schools and percentages by which the enrollments of girls surpass those of boys (statistical schools)

The differences are considerably less in the reorganized schools than in the regular schools, their respective percentages being, for the first year, 61.6 and 66.2; second year, 77.7 and 79.2; third year, 60.3 and 97; and fourth year, 84.4 and 93.

7. SUMMARY

From the data presented the following conclusions, which will answer the questions set forth in the beginning of this chapter, may safely be drawn: First, colored children are showing remarkable avidity in the manner in which they are embracing the secondary-school facilities provided them; second, they still show a bias toward academic curriculums but are also embracing the advantages offered in general curriculums; third, the holding power of the Negro high schools as represented by the percentages of pupils who graduate is not as strong as it should be as compared with the white schools; fourth, the power to stimulate in pupils a continuing interest in education after graduation is very pronounced; finally, there appears to be a strong tendency in favor of educating colored girls.

CHAPTER VII : TEACHERS AND PRINCIPALS

1. THE TEACHERS

The concern of the chapter.—In Chapters II and III certain general facts were presented regarding the number and compensation of 5,040 Negro public high-school teachers in the schools of the Southern States; in Chapter V the offering of these schools, as one of the educational agencies, was discussed, and in Chapter VI the pupil, as the central factor in the whole educational scheme was treated from the viewpoint of his general relation to the school and its offerings. The burden of the present chapter is to present evidence concerning the instructional staff whose function it is to make the school an effective educational agency.

In order to know to what extent effectiveness may be expected of teachers and officers, it is necessary to know several things about them. How much of a job is committed to their hands? How well have they been prepared for their task? What experience have they had in developing skills and techniques? And, finally, what monetary rewards do they receive? It is the purpose of this chapter to present data which will help answer these questions.

The Secondary Survey inquiry form to Negro high schools contained very few questions relating to teachers, inasmuch as it was deemed more feasible, and probably more accurate, to utilize the data secured from personnel questionnaires returned by Negro high-school teachers to the National Survey of the Education of Teachers. Therefore, unless otherwise indicated, the facts presented on teachers in this section have reference to teachers participating in the Survey just mentioned.

Teaching load.—Several factors enter into the determination of the load a teacher carries. The only ones considered in this study are (1) the subject-matter fields in which teaching is done, (2) the hours per week taught, and (3) the number of pupils per teacher.

Number of subject fields.—Closely related courses are grouped into what is known as a subject field. For example,

[66]

courses offered in arithmetic, general mathematics, algebra, plane and solid geometry, and trigonometry are all classified under the general grouping or subject field, mathematics.

From Table 27 it will be seen that more than half the teachers reporting instruct in two subject fields, the percentage being 56. A fifth of the teachers must prepare lessons in three or more fields. Only 32 per cent of the teachers in unselected 4-year high schools for whites [1] teach in two subject fields, and less than 2 per cent must prepare lessons in as many as three or more fields.

Teaching combinations.—It is not enough to know merely the number of different fields in which a teacher must give instruction in order to understand the teaching load. It is necessary to know also the nature of the teaching combinations. Table 28 presents this information. Of the 1,282 teachers replying to this question, 949 claimed to have a second main field of teaching, distributed in the combinations listed. The rank of the six principal subject fields taught by the greatest number of persons who also have a second main field of teaching, with the number of teachers involved, follows: English, 307; mathematics, 181; social science, 123; biology, 90; physical science, 76; and classical languages, 57.

TABLE 27.—*Numbers and percentages of teachers in high schools for Negro and white children giving instruction in the different numbers of subject fields*

Number of subject fields	Negro teachers [a]	White teachers [b]	Negro per cent of total	White per cent of total
1	2	3	4	5
1	323	751	25. 2	48. 4
2	720	493	56. 1	31. 7
3	127	219	9. 9	14. 1
4	74	74	5. 8	4. 8
5	27	12	2. 1	.8
6	10	2	.8	.1
7	1	2	.1	.1
Total	1, 282	1, 553	100. 0	100. 0

[a] National Survey of the Education of Teachers.
[b] Monograph No. 6.

[1] Monograph No. 6. Op. cit.

TABLE 28.—*Number of teachers who give instruction in the subject fields specified below in addition to their principal fields of teaching* [1]

Principal field of teaching	Total in subject fields	Second main field of teaching																Total
		Agriculture	Art	Biology	Business	Education	English	Classical language	Modern language	Health and physical education	Home economics	Physical science	Mathematics	Music	Social science	Trades and industries	Others	
1	2	3	4	5	6	7	8	9	10	11	12	13	14	15	16	17	18	19
Agriculture	13			3			2			1			1		4	1		12
Art	14						4			1			1	1	3			10
Biology	109	2	1		2	2	9	1	2	6	1	28	14	1	18	3		90
Business	8			2			1						3		1			7
Education	19	1		1	2		2	1	1	1		1	2		2			14
English	415		2	19		24		22	31	9		6	56	15	121	1	1	307
Classical language	72		1		1	1	17		10	2		1	8	3	13			57
Modern language	45		1		1	1	14	5		4		3	2	1	9			41
Health and physical education	20					1	1	1			1	1	2	1	8	1		17
Home economics	12			1			2					1	1		1			6
Physical science	97	1		30	1	1	2	1	1	2	2		21	4	10			76
Mathematics	247	3	1	19	2	13	33	12	9	10	1	34		2	37	2	3	181
Music	8					1	1	1	1				1					5
Social science	192	1		7	4	10	46	8	7	8	6	8	5	7		2	4	123
Trade and industry	4												1					1
Others	7						1								1			2
Total	1,282	8	6	82	13	54	135	52	62	44	11	83	118	35	228	10	8	949

[1] National Survey of the Education of Teachers.

The subject fields which were cited as the second main fields of teaching, ranked according to frequency of mention, are as follows: Social studies, 228; English, 135; mathematics, 118; physical science, 83; biology, 82; modern languages, 62; education, 54; classical languages, 52; health and physical education, 44; music, 35; business, 13; home economics 11; trades and industries, 10; agriculture, 8; and art, 6.

Some of the combinations most frequently recurring and their frequencies are: English and social studies, 121; English and mathematics, 56; mathematics and social studies, 37; mathematics and physical science, 34; physical science and biology, 30. This table also reveals a number of peculiar subject combinations; for example, agriculture and English; English and mathematics; art and physical education; biology and business; business and classical languages; mathematics and agriculture; and mathematics and music.

While it is conceded that some persons are prepared to teach at the high-school level in subject fields so unrelated as are these, certainly the wide differences in subject matter must in many instances add greatly to the load of the teacher and make for inefficiency of instruction.

Load in clock hours per week—(a) by sex.—According to information secured from the National Survey of the Education of Teachers concerning the teaching load of Negro high-school teachers in terms of clock hours per week by sex, very little difference is found, the medians being 28.7 for men, and 29.2 for women. The range for each is from the lowest step, 1 to 9 hours per week, to the highest, more than 35 hours. The median number of hours per week taught by white teachers in unselected high schools for the country as a whole is 20.[2]

(b) By teaching field.—In terms of teaching load by field of instruction the differences in median clock hours per week are also very slight, ranging from 28.3 in classical languages to 31.8 in education. In some fields too few cases were reported for the working of reliable medians.

(c) By size of community.—The same similarity between the ranges and medians in clock hours taught per week exists when compared on the basis of size of community.

---

[2] Monograph No. 6. Op. cit.

Here the ranges in median clock hours per week are from 28.7 in cities having populations of more than 100,000 to 30.7 in cities with populations ranging from 10,000 to 99,999.

While teachers in different subject fields and in communities of different sizes may carry an approximately equal load in terms of clock hours taught per week, it should be remembered that this does not necessarily imply an equal amount of work. Many factors tend to increase or decrease the actual load of teachers in different subjects, some being determined by the nature of the subject, method of teaching, year placement of courses, and experience of teacher in the particular field.

Similarly, consideration should be given to the load in communities of various sizes. From the viewpoint of clock hours taught the teachers in the open country and the villages appear to be placed at no particular disadvantage in comparison with their fellow teachers in the larger places. This is not, however, the case. Teachers in the smaller schools located in the open country and villages, because of the smallness of the teaching staff, are required to teach in a larger number of subject fields and more courses within a field, which increases to some extent the complexity of the teacher's tasks.

Pupil-teacher ratio.—In the preceding section attention was called to inadequacy of clock hours taught per week as a true measure of the teaching load. Likewise, the average number of pupils taught can not alone give a true picture of the load carried. This is shown in Table 29. From the facts presented it appears that the teachers in the smaller schools have a great advantage over those in the larger schools, but it should be kept in mind that, although teachers in Groups A and B have a smaller number of pupils to teach, they must teach a greater variety of subjects and courses. In all probability most of the unusual subject combinations mentioned earlier in this chapter will be found in the smaller schools.

Extent of training.—The extent of training of Negro high-school teachers will be considered under four heads, namely, (a) highest level of training attained, (b) degrees held and their sources, (c) credits earned in principal field of teaching, and (d) credits earned in education or professional subjects.

TABLE 29.—*Teaching load of colored and white high-school teachers according to number of pupils per teacher, by size and type of school* [1]

Pupil teacher ratio	Size group						Type	
	A	B	C	D	E	F	Reor-ganized	Regu-lar
1	2	3	4	5	6	7	8	9
Colored_____	14.5	19.7	32.4	28.5	32.1	32.8	30.4	24.9
White_____	9.2	12.7	16.1	19.8	25.5	_____	_____	_____

[1] The data for colored teachers were secured from the statistical group of schools; those for whites, from the unselected 4-year schools, reported in Monograph No. 6.

TABLE 30.—*Distribution of teachers in Negro high schools according to the highest level of training attained, by size of community and by sex (National Survey of the Education of Teachers)*

Level of training	Size of place						Sex	
	Open coun-try	Vil-lages of less than 2,500	Cities 2,500 to 9,999	Cities 10,000 to 99,999	Cities of more than 100,000	Total	Men	Women
1	2	3	4	5	6	7	8	9
1 year of high school_____	_____	1	_____	_____	_____	1	_____	1
2 years of high school_____	_____	_____	1	1	_____	2	_____	2
3 years of high school_____	4	1	2	_____	2	9	1	9
4 years of high school_____	18	3	5	11	2	39	5	34
6 to 12 weeks of college_____	8	4	3	2	1	18	4	14
Half year of college_____	5	3	_____	_____	_____	8	_____	8
1 year of college_____	9	3	9	15	9	45	4	42
2 years of college_____	13	18	33	34	48	146	25	123
3 years of college_____	9	20	17	40	36	122	23	99
4 years of college_____	40	98	122	267	350	877	382	499
1 year of graduate work_____	3	6	9	22	68	108	54	54
2 years of graduate work_____	_____	1	3	5	20	29	20	9
3 years of graduate work_____	_____	1	_____	2	7	10	8	2
More than 3 years of graduate work_	_____	_____	1	1	2	4	4	_____
Total_____	109	159	205	400	545	1,418	530	896
Median years of college training____	2.8	4.3	4.3	4.4	4.5	4.4	4.5	4.2

(a) *Highest level of training.*—The distribution of teachers according to the highest levels of training attained by size of community and sex is reported in Table 30. The median level of training of men and women in years of college training is nearly equal, being, respectively, 4.5 and 4.2. The median for the total group giving usable answers on the basis of size of place is 4.4. A slight increase in the amount of college training may be observed as the size of community increases. Assuming that the training of teachers is an index of educational opportunity, the children in the open country, where the lowest median is found, are at a marked disadvantage as compared with those in villages and larger centers of population.

(b) *Degrees held.*—As revealed by Table 31, of the 1,434 teachers replying concerning education, 994 hold bachelors' degrees, 63 masters' degrees, and 5 the degree of doctor of philosophy. Those holding degrees represent 69 per cent of all who reported on level of training. It should be borne in mind that no attempt was made to investigate the value of training attained. This is largely determined by the standards of the institutions in which credits and degrees were earned.

A feature of interest in this table is the large percentage of teachers who received their degrees from private colleges or universities. This is important when considered in connection with the fact that all teachers reporting in this study are public-school teachers. It emphasizes the importance of the place which private schools still maintain in the education of the colored people.

(c) *Training in subjects taught.*—Inasmuch as a large proportion of the teachers give instruction in more than one subject field, special interest attaches to the amount of preparation they have had in the fields in which they teach. It is generally known that many persons are required to teach subjects for which they have had little or no preparation. However, this investigation did not go beyond ascertaining data on the preparation of teachers in the field in which they do most of their teaching. Medians were computed only for those subject fields for which numbers of teachers were large enough to give reliable results. The order of the subject fields in amount of training possessed by teachers, from highest to lowest, is as follows: Modern language, physical sciences, biology, social studies, English, mathematics, and classical languages. However, the differences among the subject fields are not particularly notable.

TABLE 31.—*Numbers and percentages of teachers in Negro high schools holding degrees from various sources (National Survey of the Education of Teachers)*

Source of degrees	Degrees					
	Bachelor's		Master's		Doctor's	
	Number	Per cent	Number	Per cent	Number	Per cent
1	2	3	4	5	6	7
State or city teachers college	41	4	2	3		
Private teachers college	10	1	2	3		
State college for women					1	
City college or university			5	8	3	
State university or land-grant college	204	21	17	27	1	
Other State-supported institution	43	4				
Private college or university	24	2				
	672	68	37	59		
Total	994	69	63	4	5	0.3

(d) *Training in the field of education.*—The regulations for certification of most of the States require a certain minimum of training in the special field of education. Despite these requirements a considerable number of persons are teaching in Negro high schools with a negligible amount of training along this line. According to findings in the National Survey of the Education of Teachers, 13 per cent of the 1,208 Negro high-school teachers replying to the question concerning credits in education had from zero to 12 semester hours credit; 32 per cent had from 13 to 24 semester hours of such training, while 54 per cent had as much as 25 hours or more. The median number of semester hours in education for the whole group is 26.8.

Practice teaching.—Another important element in the professional preparation of teachers is practice teaching. Of the 852 Negro high-school teachers replying to questions concerning this element, 13 per cent reported no credit; 23.4 per cent reported 1 to 3 semester hours; 25.7 per cent, 4 to 6 hours; 16 per cent, 7 to 12 hours; 8 per cent, 13 to 18 hours; and 13.8 per cent, more than 18 hours. The median number of semester hours in practice teaching for the entire group is 6.3.

Experience.—The distribution by years of experience of teachers according to level of training is shown in Table 32. It will be noted that the median years of experience for the whole group of 1,393 teachers is seven. It is of special significance to note that 785, or 56 per cent, of these teachers had more than five years of experience as compared with 36 per cent of the white teachers in the unselected 4-year high schools, reported in Monograph No. 6. Another feature of importance in this table is the length of experience of those teachers having the lowest level of training.

TABLE 32.—*Distribution of teachers in Negro high schools according to the years of experience and level of training (National Survey of the Education of Teachers)*

| Years of experience | Level of training | | | | Total |
	4 years of high school or less	6 weeks to 2 years of college	3 to 4 years of college	1 year or more of graduate work	
1	**2**	**3**	**4**	**5**	**6**
1	4	12	94	3	113
2	5	7	110	8	130
3	3	12	111	8	134
4	2	16	89	9	116
5	3	13	89	10	115
6	3	15	57	13	88
7	3	9	59	9	80
8	4	9	40	12	65
9		10	26	6	42
10		9	25	8	42
11–15	6	29	94	28	157
16–20	6	28	80	21	135
21–25	2	15	58	5	80
26–30	5	13	27	5	50
31–35		10	5	2	17
More than 35	5	5	15	4	29
Total	51	212	979	151	1,393
Median years of experience	8.6	10.3	5.9	9.6	7.0

Salary and training.—Everyone recognizes in theory the importance of adequate salaries in promoting educational efficiency. The situation in regard to salaries of Negro teachers leaves much to be desired. In Figure 12 is shown the salary situation for Negro junior and senior high school teachers according to level of training attained. The median

[74]

salary for the whole group of 1,384 replying is $954. The median for white teachers in 4-year unselected high schools is $1,479. In the selected high schools for whites the median is $1,601.[3] It is to be remembered that these selected and unselected high schools are not located exclusively in the Southern States. A more highly desirable comparison would be with median salaries of white high-school teachers reporting in the National Survey of the Education of Teachers from the same States in which the Negro high-school teachers are located. A difference in arrangement of data, however,

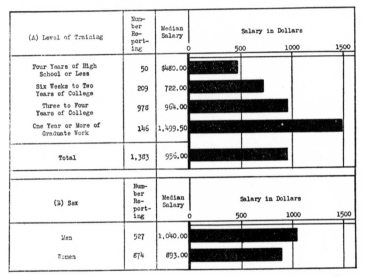

FIGURE 12.—Median salaries of Negro junior and senior high school teachers according to level of training and by sex (National Survey of the Education of Teachers)

makes direct comparisons impossible. Some indication of the divergencies which exist may be suggested by the following facts:

The range of median salaries of whites is from $921 for female junior high school teachers employed for 9 months in Alabama to $2,943 for male senior high school teachers employed for 10 months in Missouri.[4] Thus it is seen that in terms of State medians the lowest median salary of white

[3] Monograph No. 6. op. cit.
[4] National Survey of the Education of Teachers.

[75]

high-school teachers is only slightly less than the median salary of all Negro high-school teachers, while the highest median salary of whites is more than three times as great as the median salary for colored teachers.

One significant feature in this figure to which particular attention is called is the apparent influence of training on salary. According to these data low training and low salary and high training and high salary have a strong tendency to go together; as one increases, the other also increases. No attempt is made here to suggest which one is cause and which is result. As is observable, there is a difference of five or more years between the first and fourth levels of training. The difference between the median salaries of these levels is $1,019.24.

Salary and sex.—In Figure 12 are shown also the salaries of Negro men and women who teach in high schools, the medians being, respectively, $1,086 and $895.

Salaries by size and type of school.—The size of school has a decided influence on the salary the teacher is likely to receive. Table 33 shows the distribution of Negro high-school teachers by size of salary during 1929–30 and by size and type of school. The salary ($1,366.66) of the typical teacher in Group VI, the largest size of school, is 149 per cent greater than the salary ($547.96) of the typical teacher in Group I, the smallest size of school. Likewise, wide variation exists in the salaries of teachers in regular and reorganized schools, the difference being 37 per cent in favor of the latter.

A great difference is also apparent between the salaries of colored teachers and of white teachers in selected and unselected schools, the greatest difference being in the smaller schools. Although not demonstrated in the table, the median salary of white teachers of Group I is $686, (or 125 per cent) greater than the median for Negro teachers in the corresponding group. The differences between the white and colored teachers' salaries in regular and reorganized schools, respectively, are $709 (or 80 per cent) and $362 (or 30 per cent) in favor of the whites.[5]

---

[5] Ibid.

TABLE 33.—*Distribution of Negro high-school teachers by size of salary during 1929–30 and by size and type of school (Survey schools)*

Schools	Salary in dollars											Negro teachers		White teachers [1]	
	200 or less	201 to 400	401 to 600	601 to 800	801 to 1,000	1,001 to 1,200	1,201 to 1400	1,401 to 1,600	1,601 to 1,800	1,801 to 2,000	More than 2,000	Median	Number reporting	Median	Number reporting
1	2	3	4	5	6	7	8	9	10	11	12	13	14	15	16
Size groups:															
I	5	27	66	28	27	2	4	2				$547.96	161	$1,233	123
II	5	19	55	64	39	7	16					674.44	205	1,316	188
III			71	112	93	4	33	10	10	4		775.10	337	1,383	344
IV			22	48	83		36	13	24	1		905.81	227	1,482	522
V			5	13	38	24	21			3	22	1,076.00	126	1,668	683
VI				47	56	28	99	18	16	45	230	1,366.66	539		
Type:															
Regular	8	35	141	208	275	52	116	34	17	8	140	891.90	1,034	1,601	459
Reorganized	2	11	78	104	61	13	93	9	33	45	112	1,225.73	561	1,588	556
Total	10	46	219	312	336	65	209	43	50	53	252	926.29	1,595	1,479	1,860
Per cent of teachers	0.6	2.8	13.7	19.5	21.0	4.0	13.1	2.6	3.1	3.3	15.7				

[1] Monograph No. 6. Op. cit. Data on salaries of white teachers according to size groups obtained from the unselected 4-year high schools. Data on salaries of white teachers by type of school obtained from selected high schools.

2. THE PRINCIPALS

The importance of the principal.—The administrative head of any organization or institution must be regarded as important to its success. This is obviously true of principals of high schools. Upon the principal rests the responsibility of educational leadership and coordination.

The principal of the Negro high school is charged with an unusual trust. Frequently he is considered the leading Negro in the community. Because of the lack of professional advancement often found among Negro teachers he is not subjected to the critical scrutiny prevalent in a more highly professionalized atmosphere. In many places the needs and problems of the white schools consume the major portion of the superintendent's time; consequently, he relies largely on the recommendations and opinions of the Negro principal in matters affecting Negro schools, sometimes without subjecting those recommendations and opinions to critical and personal inquiry. All these conditions tend to surround the Negro principal with considerable power and authority, and place upon him a heavy responsibility.

It is important, therefore, to know something of the general status of the principal of the Negro high school, as well as certain details concerning his training, experience, the distribution of his time, and his remuneration. This section attempts to reveal these facts. All the data on the principal were secured from the Survey schools.

Sex and marital status.—This study shows that of the 399 principals replying to this question 31 are women and 368 are men. A third of the women and four-fifths of the men are married. The percentage of both men and women combined who are married is 81. The corresponding percentage for white teachers in unselected schools is 82.7.

Ages.—The median age of the 348 men replying is 42.4 years; of the 24 women replying, 40.5. The range for men is from 22 to 77; for women, from 25 to 65.

Training by size and type of school.—In general the amount of training possessed by principals in the larger sized schools is greater than that possessed by those in the smaller schools, the medians being 4.0 years above high school for principals of schools in size Group I; 4.3 for principals in Group II; 4.4 for those in Group III; 4.9 for those in Group IV; 5.6 for those in Group V; and 5.9 for those in Group VI.

The training of principals of reorganized and regular schools is, respectively, 4.4 and 4.6 years of collegiate training.

The percentage of Negro high-school principals having less than four years of training beyond high school is 22.2 as compared with 3.6 for whites.[6] Negro and white principals having more than five years of training beyond high school are practically the same, the respective percentages being 12.9 and 12.2.

Table 34 shows the number of principals holding certain degrees according to size of school. The percentages of principals holding certain degrees are for colored and white, respectively: Bachelor's, 83 and 75; master's, 16 and 24; doctor's 0.6 and 0.7.

---

[6] Ibid.

[78]

TABLE 34.—*Distribution of principals of high schools for Negroes according to degrees held and by size and type of school*

Degree	Size group						Regu-lar	Reor-gan-ized	Total Negro	Total white[1]
	I	II	III	IV	V	VI				
1	2	3	4	5	6	7	8	9	10	11
Bachelor's:										
Number	75	65	61	31	8	17	203	54	257	327
Per cent	96	93	77	81.5	61.5	53	86.3	72	83	75
Master's:										
Number	3	5	18	7	4	14	32	19	51	105
Per cent	3.8	7	22.7	18.4	30.7	43.7	13.6	25.3	16	24
Doctor's:										
Number						1	1		2	3
Per cent						7.6	3		2.6	0.6	0.7
Total schools re-porting	78	70	79	38	13	32	235	75	310	435

[1] Data from Monograph No. 6.

Professional training.—The professional training of principals in semester hours of credit in the field of education is higher than that for teachers, the respective medians being 31.5 and 26.8. Although the median number of semester hours of professional training of principals of schools in size Group II is slightly less than that for principals in Group I, the general trend is upward as the size of the school increases. The respective medians are: For Group I, 29.4; Group II, 27.8; Group III, 31.8; Group IV, 36.5; Group V, 37.3; and Group VI, 39. The medians for Negro principals of regular and reorganized schools are, respectively, 31.9 and 30. The medians for white principals of selected regular and reorganized schools are, respectively, 32.5 and 38.7. For the white principals of unselected 4-year high schools the median hours for the total number are 30.2. Medians for white principals in each size group are: I, 24.8; II, 25.1; III, 33.9; IV, 35.3; V, 37.[7]

Summer school attendance.—One very important criterion by which the professional advancement of educators is judged is attendance in summer schools. To secure information on this point principals were asked to designate the year in which they last attended summer school. Replies to this question gave the following significant results: 94.5 per cent of principals in Group I had attended summer school during the past 5 years; 97.1 in Group II; 89.7 in Group III;

[7] Ibid.

92.1 in Group IV; 93.3 in Group V; and 77.4 in Group VI. The fact that relatively fewer principals of large city high schools have attended summer school during the past 5 years may lead to the assumption that this is a result of a greater initial amount of academic and professional training. However, the training of principals in Groups IV and V is not sufficiently far below that of principals in Group VI to warrant the differential of 15.9 per cent in the number attending summer school within the past 5 years.

The length of time since all principals combined attended summer school and the percentages attending within a given period follow. During the year of report, 53.9; 1 year earlier, 17.2; 2 years, 9.6; 3 years, 5.3; 4 years, 5.9; 5 to 9 years, 5.3; 10 to 14 years, 0.8; 15 to 19 years, 1.1; 20 years or more, 0.5.

Experience and tenure.—If experience is important for a teacher it is all the more so for a principal. The complexity of the problems which he is called on to solve requires a finesse which can only come, if at all, with experience. How much educational experience have the principals of schools for colored children had, and how long have they been in their present positions? Figure 13 supplies data for answering these questions. Three hundred and seventy-six principals replied concerning experience, and 386 concerning tenure in present position.

(a) *Experience.*—With the exception of the schools in size Group VI, a progressive increase in median years of experience of Negro high-school principals is noted in Figure 13 as the size of school increases. The median for Group VI is, nevertheless, greater than that of Group IV. The median for Group V is almost twice as great as for Group I. The differences between the experience of principals of regular and reorganized schools seem not to be significant, their respective medians being 16.7 and 18.3 years. The median for all principals combined is 17.3.

An important feature about this diagram is the contrast between the experience of colored and white principals. In nearly all size groups the median of colored principals is twice that of white principals, and in some cases even more. This is in agreement with the findings concerning teachers reported in the first section of the chapter.

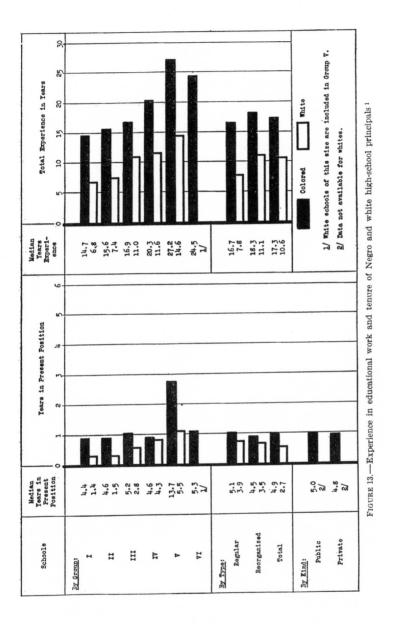

FIGURE 13.—Experience in educational work and tenure of Negro and white high-school principals [1]

---

[1] Data on white principals from Monograph No. 6, The Smaller Secondary Schools.

(b) *Tenure.*—Excessive turnover of staff is a weak point in school administration. What is the situation regarding turnover for Negro high-school principals? According to Figure 13, the median number of years all principals have been in their present positions is 5.9. No significant differences are shown among the different size groups, except in Group V, which, as was true in the median years of experience, has a median considerably higher than the others. The differences between regular and reorganized and private and public schools also are slight. Again, in every instance, the median of Negro principals exceeds that of white principals. For the total groups it is 2.7 for whites, and 5.9 for Negroes.

Caution should be exercised in concluding that this excess of experience and length of tenure is always constructive in influence. The converse may often be true.

Distribution of the principal's time.—The effectiveness with which a principal functions in his position of educational leadership will depend on the manner in which his time is distributed to his various duties. Assuming that his efficiency as a principal, other things being equal, is in inverse ratio to the amount of teaching he does, the facts in Figure 14 present an unfavorable picture.

Teaching responsibilities.—As will be seen in Figure 14, the smaller the school the heavier the teaching load of the principal. A rapid decrease in median number of hours devoted to teaching is apparent as the size of school increases. The medians for Groups V and VI are not shown because the numbers involved were too small to insure reliability.

The difference between the regular and the reorganized schools in the median number of hours devoted to teaching is not great, but the medians themselves are large, being almost equal to the median of the small schools in Group II. The median for the total group of 267 principals replying to this inquiry is 17.5.

Supervision.—Supervision of instruction should be a principal's chief function, but, according to facts shown in Figure 14, he devotes only a small portion of his time to this important task. The amount of time, however, increases with the size of school. For the 240 principals reporting on this item, the median is 7.1 hours per week.

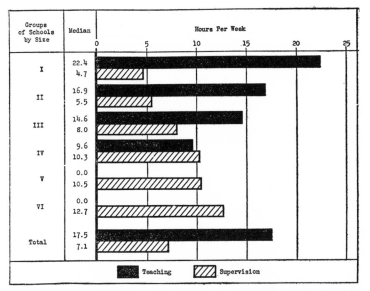

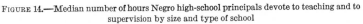

FIGURE 14.—Median number of hours Negro high-school principals devote to teaching and to supervision by size and type of school

Assistance to principal.—Another important factor affecting a principal's ability to perform the larger duties devolving upon him is the assistance he has in discharging the more simple matters of routine. In Table 35 is shown the number of principals who have certain additional administrative and supervisory assistance. More than a third of the principals reported assistant or vice principals, the percentage being 36.1. In view of the increasing importance of guidance and student personnel work it is significant to note that only 7.3 per cent of the principals reported directors of guidance.

TABLE 35.—*Numbers and percentages of Negro high-school principals who have the assistance of certain additional administrative and supervisory functionaries*

Officer	Num-ber	Per cent	Officer	Num-ber	Per cent
Assistant or vice principal	152	36.1	Regular clerical assistance	75	17.8
Dean of girls	81	19.2	Regular clerical assistance to department heads	3	.7
Dean of boys	50	11.8			
Registrar	67	15.9	Student clerical assistance to principal	58	13.7
Home-room advisor	89	21.1			
Counselors or advisors	45	10.6	Student clerical assistance to department heads	17	4.0
Directors of guidance	31	7.3			
Heads of departments	90	21.3	Others	16	3.8
Supervisors of instruction	26	6.1			

Salaries.—Whatever else may be cited as important in stimulating and aiding principals and teachers to be progressive, remuneration still remains one of the most potent factors. This should prompt some interest in the salaries of principals of Negro high schools. Figure 15 compares the median salaries of colored and white high school principals. It also shows the percentages of colored principals receiving salaries within given ranges. The contrast between these

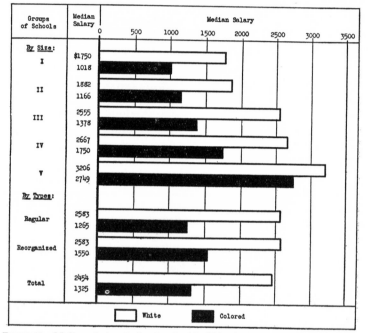

FIGURE 15.—Median salaries of colored and white high-school principals according to size and type of school

salaries is striking. For this study colored principals in Group VI were combined with those in Group V to make the range comparable to Group V for the white principals.

Of the 372 Negro high-school principals for whom data were gathered, 61.2 per cent receive annual salaries of less than $1,500, while only 7.6 per cent of the salaries of the 430 white principals of unselected schools fell below this amount.

3. SUMMARY

Negro secondary-school teachers were found to carry a heavy load in terms of number of different subject fields taught and of pupil-teacher ratio. They had had a fair degree of academic and professional training as measured, respectively, by degrees held and semester-hour credits. Many, however, have meager training in the subject of their main field of teaching.

Their length of experience is greater than that of teachers in schools for white pupils. The salaries of Negro secondary teachers are small, especially in the smaller schools, and are extremely low when compared with the salaries of white teachers.

The typical principal of the Negro high school is a married man of mature years. He has attended college approximately 4½ years and has had a considerable amount of professional training. As with the Negro high-school teacher, his median experience of 17.3 years is longer than that of white principals. He has been in his present position longer, the respective medians being 2.7 for whites, and 5.9 for Negroes. Much of his time is devoted to teaching, a factor which is greatly influenced by the size of school. His median salary of $1,325 is only slightly more than half the median salary of white principals.

CHAPTER VIII : CERTAIN PRACTICES IN ADMINISTRATION AND SUPERVISION

1. HOUSING OF SECONDARY PUPILS

The concern of the chapter.—It is through good administrative and supervisory policies and practices that the school organization attains the purpose for which it was designed; that the curriculum is made to accomplish the object for which it was constructed; that the pupil is brought into such relation with the school that his education shall be an integrated whole; and that the activities of staff members are so coordinated and encouraged that a smooth working system shall result.

To what extent secondary schools for Negroes have certain practices in administration and supervision will be shown in the present chapter. No attempt has been made to round out a complete study of such problems and practices; rather, the aim has been to select some of those procedures which seemed to be of greatest significance.

Extent to which building is shared.—One of the most vexatious problems facing high-school principals is the necessity of housing secondary pupils with those of other school units. The difference in the ages of pupils, the objectives of education at the various levels, and the methods of administering the various units make it almost impossible for either unit to do its best work when more than one school must be housed in the same building.

The percentages of colored and white schools sharing their buildings with other school units are shown in Table 36. Of the 407 colored schools, 331, or 81. 3 per cent, reported other school units in their buildings. Of the 498 white schools, only 239, or 47.9 per cent, are so handicapped. There is a gradual decrease in the percentage of Negro high schools sharing buildings as the size of school increases. For the white schools this decline is rather rapid, falling as low as 13.7 per cent in the largest group.

Provision for surplus enrollment.—In order to ascertain what provision is made to care for the excessive enrollments, a condition which is frequently found among schools for colored children, principals were asked to indicate the means used in such cases. From the replies there appear to be 196, or 46.5 per cent, of the schools included in the study which have excessive enrollments. Provisions for surplus enrollments with the percentages of principals using them follow: Shortened periods, 13.5; platoon plan, 9; temporary classrooms, 26.3; other, 4.9.

TABLE 36.—*Comparison of Negro and white high schools sharing their buildings with other school units, by size and type of school* [1]

	Size groups						Type		Total
	I	II	III	IV	V	VI	Regular	Reorganized	
1	2	3	4	5	6	7	8	9	10
Number of Negro schools	113	73	82	33	12	18	255	76	331
Per cent	89.6	84.8	81.1	76.7	70.5	52.9	84.4	72.3	81.3
Per cent of white schools sharing buildings	73.6	76.0	51.8	40.5	13.7				47.9

[1] Data on white schools from Monograph No. 6.

2. RECORDS

Permanent scholarship records.—Another feature of schools for Negroes that can be said to be in need of modernization is the matter of keeping permanent records. The methods in use reported by the 414 schools replying, together with the percentages of frequency of mention, are as follows: None, 1.4; card system, 64.1; bound volume, 23.2; loose-leaf record book, 37.2; American Council Cumulative Record folder, 2.6; other, 4.2. No attempt was made to determine with what degree of effectiveness the various systems were used. That a few schools are beginning to use such modern means for keeping pupils' records as the cumulative record folder designed by the American Council on Education is an encouraging sign. A few schools employed more than one method of record keeping.

Personnel records.—Student personnel research and administration are rapidly coming into use in institutions of higher learning. The success of this movement, however, will depend largely on the type of personnel records which can be secured from schools at the lower level and the cooperation received from them. It is heartening, therefore, to note the number of schools keeping records in addition to the conventional ones on some of the more important personnel factors. The numbers and percentages of colored and white schools claiming to have records on certain characteristics are shown in Table 37. The contrast between the percentages of the white and colored schools keeping records on these items suggests the extent to which the colored schools are lagging behind in this regard.

TABLE 37.—*Numbers and percentages of colored and white high schools having records of certain student personnel factors* [1]

Factor	Colored		White	
	Number	Per cent	Number	Per cent
1	2	3	4	5
Personal traits	53	23.1	112	30.0
Interests or hobbies	46	20.0	116	31.1
Scholarship	160	69.8	328	87.9
Intelligence or psychological scores	70	30.5	222	59.5
Health	119	51.9	241	64.6
Home conditions [2]	64	27.9		
Paternal occupation	187	81.6	290	77.7
Maternal occupation [2]	170	74.2		
Pupils' vocational plans	66	28.8	175	46.9
Pupils' educational plans	60	26.2	180	48.3
Age-grade distribution [2]	101	44.1		
Residence of drop-outs and graduates [2]	98	42.7		
Occupation of drop-outs	47	20.5	[3] 94	[3] 20.4
Occupation of graduates	103	44.9	[3] 143	31.0
Total schools replying	229	54.3		

[1] Data on white schools from Monograph No. 6. (373 schools reporting.)
[2] Data not available for white schools.
[3] General information concerning drop-outs and graduates. (460 schools reporting for drop-outs and 462 schools reporting for graduates.)

The discrepancy between the facts regarding scholarship records in Table 37 and those discussed in the previous paragraph concerning permanent records probably indicates that some principals did not understand the question to apply to academic scholarship.

Another recent Office of Education study presents a mass of data concerning the need of more and better student records for use in properly placing and guiding students.[1]

3. CERTAIN MODERN PROCEDURES

Promotion.—Report here is made regarding only a limited number of procedures commonly considered representative of modern practices. In Table 37 are shown facts regarding methods of promotion, and the use of psychological and standardized tests.

As to methods of promotion, there is a sharp decline as the size of school increases in the percentage of schools promoting by grade; conversely, the percentage of schools promoting by subjects rises rapidly with the increase in size of school. Relatively fewer reorganized schools than regular schools promote by grade.

Psychological and standardized tests.—It will be observed in Table 38 that a larger percentage of the large schools give psychological and standardized examinations and tests and also use their results than of the smaller schools. The differences in the percentages of schools giving psychological and standardized examinations and using them are in favor of the reorganized schools.

Among the unselected 4-year high schools for white children, it was found that the percentages of schools in each size-group giving intelligence tests[2] are as follows: Group I, 36.1; II, 44.6; III, 51.8; IV, 61.3; V, 58.9. In each group the percentage of white schools giving intelligence tests exceeds that for the colored schools. For all groups combined the percentages for whites and Negroes, respectively, are 51.9 and 36.1.

---

[1] Caliver, Ambrose. A Background Study of Negro College Students. Washington, Government Printing Office, 1933. (U. S. Office of Education, Bulletin, 1933, No. 8.)

[2] The term "intelligence tests" used here carries the same meaning as "psychological examinations" used in the preceding paragraph.

TABLE 38.—*Numbers and percentages of Negro junior and senior high school principals employing certain modern procedures, by size and type of school*

Group	Total reporting	Methods of promotion			Psychological examination		Achievement tests		Other tests [1]	Total administering all types of tests
		By Grades	By subjects	Both	Administering	Using results	Administering	Using results	Administering	
1	2	3	4	5	6	7	8	8	10	11

BY SIZE

I:

Number	118	63	52	3	38	19	32	21	6	54
Per cent	93.6	50.0	41.2	2.3	30.1	15.0	25.3	16.6	4.7	42.8

II:

Number	84	37	46	1	25	17	24	19	3	41
Per cent	97.6	43.0	53.4	1.1	29.0	19.7	27.9	22.0	3.4	47.6

III:

Number	99	28	67	4	37	26	26	23	5	49
Per cent	98.0	27.7	66.3	3.9	36.6	25.7	25.7	22.7	4.9	48.5

IV:

Number	41	6	34	1	17	12	21	17	5	24
Per cent	95.3	13.9	79.0	2.3	39.5	27.9	48.8	39.5	11.6	55.8

V:

Number	17	3	14	------	8	4	7	5	------	10
Per cent	100.0	17.6	82.3	------	47.0	23.5	41.1	29.4	------	58.8

VI:

Number	33	4	29	------	22	20	18	19	4	24
Per cent	97.0	11.7	85.2	------	64.7	58.8	52.9	55.8	11.7	70.5

BY TYPE

Regular:

Number	291	108	177	6	107	69	92	68	13	149
Per cent	96.3	35.7	58.6	1.9	35.4	22.8	30.4	22.5	4.3	49.3

Reorganized:

Number	101	33	65	3	40	29	36	36	10	53
Per cent	96.1	31.4	61.9	2.8	38.0	27.6	34.2	34.2	9.5	50.4

Total:

Number	392	141	242	9	147	98	128	104	23	202
Per cent	96.3	34.6	59.4	2.2	36.1	24.0	31.4	25.5	5.7	49.6

Data not available on extent of use of results.

The white schools also surpass the colored schools in giving standardized subject-matter tests in all size groups except in Group IV. The percentages of white schools giving these tests for each of the size groups follow: Group I, 29.2; II, 31.5; III, 34.5; IV, 46.2; V, 46.7. For all groups combined the percentages are: For Negroes, 31.4; for whites, 38.6.

Use made of examinations.—The manner in which the results of examinations are utilized to promote the educational process in pupils is of more importance than the mere fact of administering the tests. It should be of interest, therefore, to inquire into what the Negro high schools do with the results of their psychological examinations and standardized tests. Table 39 answers this question. The use which most of the schools make of the psychological examination results is "classification, grouping, and placement of pupils," the percentage being 40.8. The use most frequently mentioned for standardized subject-matter tests is "remedial work," the percentage using the results of tests for this purpose being 35.5.

TABLE 39.—*Numbers and percentages of Negro principals who make certain uses of the results of their psychological examinations and standardized subject-matter tests*

Use	Psychological examination		Standardized subject-matter tests	
	Number	Per cent	Number	Per cent
1	2	3	4	5
Determining ability of pupils	19	19.3		
Classification groupings and placement	40	40.8	26	25.0
Lesson assignment	5	5.1		
Grading	5	5.1		
Diagnosing individual differences	11	11.2	18	17.3
Remedial work	16	16.3	37	35.5
Vocational guidance	9	9.1		
Comparative purposes			9	8.6
Supervisory agency			4	3.8
Promotions			12	11.5
Research			1	.9
Improving teaching			17	16.3
Other	7	7.1	4	3.8
Total principals reporting	98		104	

4. PROVISIONS FOR INDIVIDUAL DIFFERENCES

An important contribution of modern psychology to education is the establishment of the fact of individual differences. It has also stimulated the development of techniques for discovering and handling these differences. Table 40 lists the provisions which 338 of the Survey schools make for individual differences of their pupils and the frequency of use according to size and type of school.

An important conclusion from this table is the outstanding advantage which the larger schools have over the smaller ones in the percentage which attempts to care for the individual differences of their pupils. The reorganized schools also have an advantage over the regular schools in most cases,

TABLE 40.—*Numbers and percentages*[1] *of Negro junior and senior high school principals reporting the employment of certain provisions in caring for individual differences, by size and type of school*

Provision	Size groups						Type		Total schools reporting
	I	II	III	IV	V	VI	Regular	Reorganized	
1	2	3	4	5	6	7	8	9	10
Ability grouping:									
Number	41	24	27	17	7	20	103	33	136
Per cent	32.5	27.9	26.5	39.5	41.1	58.9	34.1	31.4	33
Class sectioning:									
Number	17	22	20	15	6	15	66	29	95
Per cent	13.4	25.5	19.8	34.8	35.2	44.1	21.8	27.6	23.3
Adaptation of courses to needs of sections:									
Number	32	28	40	17	3	19	95	44	139
Per cent	25.3	32.5	39.6	39.5	17.6	55.8	31.4	41.9	34.1
Variation of marking systems in different sections:									
Number	10	6	6	4	1	4	24	7	31
Per cent	7.9	6.9	5.9	9.3	5.8	11.7	7.9	6.6	7.6
Supervised study:									
Number	47	35	51	25	8	14	134	46	180
Per cent	37.3	40.6	50.4	58.1	47.0	41.1	44.3	43.8	44.2
Increased pupil load for the superior:									
Number	29	27	37	15	6	16	86	44	130
Per cent	23.0	31.3	36.6	34.8	35.2	47.0	28.4	41.9	31.9
Honor organization:									
Number	32	27	32	18	7	15	98	33	131
Per cent	25.3	31.3	31.6	41.8	41.1	44.1	32.4	31.4	32.1
Varied credit for individual achievement:									
Number	16	21	18	3	2	2	46	16	62
Per cent	12.6	24.4	17.8	6.9	11.7	5.8	15.2	15.2	15.2
Other:									
Number	1	1	2	1	-----	-----	3	2	5
Per cent	.7	1.1	1.9	2.3	-----	-----	.9	1.9	1.2
Total different schools reporting:									
Number	96	77	81	39	14	31	255	83	338
Per cent	76.1	89.5	80.1	90.6	82.3	91.1	83.6	81.3	83.0

[1] Percentages worked on total schools in each group and type excluding the 14 unclassified schools.

5. CERTAIN ADDITIONAL PROVISIONS

The efficiency of a school is no longer estimated solely by its regular classroom work for day pupils during the regular session. School people and their constituents are beginning to realize that the services of a school should extend beyond the walls of the classroom and beyond the limited range of the conventional school day. These persons believe that the school should be a vital community center, considering the needs of the unfortunate deviates as well as the normal child, and should encompass the whole life span rather than merely the period of childhood and adolescence. Table 41 shows by the percentages of schools providing for certain extended services to what extent persons who have the control and administration of colored high schools have put into operation this larger vision. The larger schools lead in offering classes for adults, extension courses, and summer schools. In the other items, however, there is considerable variation between the size groups.

TABLE 41.—*Numbers and percentages of schools making certain additional provisions for secondary-school work by size and type* [1]

Group	Summer school	Evening or night school	Part-time or continuation school	Opportunity school or class	Classes for delinquents	Classes for physically handicapped	Extension or correspondence courses	Classes for adults	Other	Total different schools replying	Percentage having some additional provision
1	2	3	4	5	6	7	8	9	10	11	12
BY SIZE											
I:											
Number	10	9	26	16	2	4		2		40	
Per cent	25.0	22.5	65.0	40.0	5.0	10.0		5.0			31.7
II:											
Number	11	7	26	10				2	2	37	
Per cent	29.7	18.9	70.2	27.0				5.4	5.4		43.0
III:											
Number	17	10	23	11	7	10		1	3	42	
Per cent	40.4	23.8	54.7	26.1	16.6	23.8		2.3	7.1		41.5
IV:											
Number	12	7	11	6	5	4	1	3	1	24	
Per cent	50.0	29.1	45.9	25.0	20.8	16.6	4.1	12.5	4.1		55.8
V:											
Number	11	2	4		2	1	2	2		13	
Per cent	84.6	15.3	30.7		15.3	7.6	15.3	15.3			76.4
VI:											
Number	20	9	16	3	3			1	2	28	
Per cent	71.4	32.1	57.1	10.7	10.7		35.7		7.1		82.3
BY TYPE											
Regular:											
Number	57	31	80	37	14	14	3	8	4	130	
Per cent	43.8	23.8	61.5	28.4	10.7	10.7	2.3	6.1	3.0		43.0
Reorganized:											
Number	24	13	26	9	5	5	1	2	4	54	
Per cent	44.4	24.0	48.1	16.6	9.2	9.2	1.8	3.7	7.4		51.4
Total:											
Number	81	44	106	46	19	19	4	10	8	184	
Per cent	44.0	23.9	57.6	25.0	10.3	10.3	2.1	5.4	4.3		45.2

[1] Includes 14 schools from border States.

Peculiar as it may seem, the regular schools surpass the reorganized schools in offering each of the provisions listed except two, which are summer schools and evening or night schools, and even here the differences are so slight as to be insignificant. Considering the percentage of schools which have additional provisions, irrespective of kind, the reorganized schools surpass the regular ones, their respective percentages being 51.4 and 43. Also, in the matter of total additional provisions, there is a progressive increase in percentages of schools having them as the size of school increases.

6. HEALTH FACILITIES

Health officers.—In view of the statistics cited in Chapter II concerning the health of the colored population, facts regarding health facilities provided in Negro high schools should be pertinent in this study. The data gathered, although informative, are meager at best, and indicative of the need for further investigation.

The percentages of Negro and white high schools according to size groups providing school nurses, physicians, and dentists are revealed in Table 42. It will be noted that the percentage of Negro schools making such provision increases as the size of school increases. A comparison of the percentages by race reveals considerable fluctuation. The total figures, however, show close similarity in the provision of school nurses and school dentists, but great difference in the provision of school physicians.

The percentages of Negro schools, according to size groups, having certain other officers, which are not shown in the table, are: Group I, 7.1; II, 18.6; III, 10.8; IV, 6.9; V, 0; and VI, 11.7. Of all the 233 schools reporting on this item 10.5 per cent had some "other" health officer.

Supervision of health.—Other provisions for health supervision and improvement, by percentages of schools employing, include: Instruction in physiology and hygiene, 63.8; required courses in physical education, 38; annual and periodical physical examination, 37; corrective exercises, 30.1; medical clinic, 23; dental clinic, 19; corrective diet, 16.8; and other, 2.4.

TABLE 42.—*Percentages of Negro (Survey) high schools and unselected white high schools having school nurses, physicians, and dentists, by size of school* [1]

Group	School nurse		School physician		School dentist	
	Negro	White	Negro	White	Negro	White
1	2	3	4	5	6	7
I	19.8	58.3	20.7	60.4	7.1	----------
II	26.7	----------	29.0	65.7	8.1	14.3
III	40.5	44.4	31.6	53.3	19.9	17.8
IV	48.8	43.8	30.2	49.4	13.9	20.2
V	64.7	41.9	58.8	42.9	35.2	16.2
VI	73.5	----------	73.5	----------	20.5	----------
Total	35.8	37.3	32.1	52.7	13.5	15.2

[1] Data for white schools from Monograph No. 6.

7. INSTRUCTION

Length of recitation.—In the final analysis most of the features discussed thus far in this report are designed to facilitate and improve instruction and learning. Although many factors enter into the instructional process, it is outside the scope of this investigation to go beyond a consideration of more than the limited number included.

The recitation period is admittedly the medium through which most instruction takes place in schools. The length of the period, therefore, is an important factor in conditioning the amount and kind of instruction that can be given. The median lengths of class periods in minutes for the 392 Survey schools replying to this question according to size and type of school are as follows: Group I, 40.7; II, 43.5; III, 43.4; IV, 47.6; V, 45.6; VI, 44.9. There is a gradual increase in the length of the typical class period as the size of school increases, but the differences are not particularly significant. Neither is the difference between the regular and reorganized schools great, their respective medians being 43.3 and 42 minutes. The median length of recitation period for all schools combined is 43.1 minutes.

Instructional procedures.—How best to adjust education to the needs of adolescent boys and girls has long been a subject of serious study by educators and psychologists. With the growing complexity of life and the increasing multiplicity of

[95]

problems facing high-school teachers, there has developed a conviction that the main object of instruction should be to develop a thinking, socialized individual. To effect this result economically has been the purpose of those who have evolved some of the new procedures and techniques of instruction. The extent to which secondary schools for Negroes have kept abreast of newer developments along this line may be seen in Table 43, if the answers which principals gave may be taken as an index. Principals were asked to indicate whether certain methods, means, and procedures were used constantly, frequently, occasionally, or not at all. Replies were tabulated both according to size and type of school and in summary form. No significant differences were found between the percentages of schools in the various size groups using the different procedures. Neither were the differences between regular and reorganized schools found to be important.

The findings of this study for all schools combined are shown in Table 43. Corresponding data for the unselected white high schools are also included. In percentages of schools using the various methods the white group far surpasses the colored group in the majority of cases. The white schools do not retain this lead, however, in the extent to which the methods are used. It will be observed that the differences between the two groups using the various methods constantly are only slight. The differences between the groups using the methods frequently are more pronounced in favor of the white schools. There is much fluctuation between the groups in the percentages of schools using the methods occasionally. Because the degrees of use are subjective rather than objective, it may be doubted that the data in Table 43 pertaining to the degrees of use have any high reliability.

8. THE LIBRARY

The facilities.—The library is increasingly becoming an important factor in the instructional process in modern schools. The number and the kinds of books provided, therefore, are important indices of the amount and quality of education available.

TABLE 43.—*Numbers and percentages of colored and white high schools employing certain methods and means of instruction* [1]

Methods and means	Constantly employed		Frequently employed		Occasionally employed		Not employed at all [2]	Total schools using various methods	
	Colored	White	Colored	White	Colored	White	Colored	Colored	White
1	2	3	4	5	6	7	8	9	10
Conventional recitation: [3]									
Number	133		85		56	144	12	274	
Per cent	32.6		20.8		13.7	30.3	2.9	67.1	
Problem method:									
Number	59	50	132	146	75	135	6	266	340
Per cent	14.4	10.5	32.4	30.7	18.4	28.4	1.4	65.2	71.6
Project in general subjects:									
Number	44	23	80	155	100	65	11	224	313
Per cent	10.8	4.8	19.6	32.6	24.5	13.6	2.7	54.9	65.9
Project in vocational work:									
Number	109	129	54	82	40	272	21	203	276
Per cent	26.7	27.1	13.2	17.2	9.8	57.2	5.1	49.7	58.1
Field trips in general subjects									
Number	27	8	46	86	163	120	11	236	366
Per cent	6.6	1.6	11.3	18.1	40.1	25.2	2.7	58.0	77.1
Field trips in vocational subjects:									
Number	37	46	51	112	75	56	29	163	278
Per cent	9.0	9.6	12.5	23.5	18.4	11.7	7.1	39.9	58.5
Use of library for instructional purposes:									
Number	187	220	78	144	35	144	15	300	420
Per cent	45.9	46.3	19.1	30.3	8.5	30.3	3.6	73.5	88.4
Use of lantern slides for instructional purposes:									
Number	12	7	31	78	43	85	88	86	229
Per cent	2.9	1.4	7.6	16.4	10.5	17.8	21.6	21.0	48.2
Use of moving pictures for instructional purposes:									
Number	5	3	8	31	64	221	75	77	119
Per cent	1.2	0.6	1.9	6.5	15.7	46.5	18.4	18.8	25.1
Observation and study of local occupations, institutions, etc.:									
Number	19	15	39	83	116	68	22	174	319
Per cent	4.6	3.1	9.5	17.4	28.5	14.3	5.4	42.6	67.2
Supervised study:									
Number	147	184	91	135	31	28	7	269	387
Per cent	36.1	38.7	22.3	28.4	7.6	5.8	1.7	66.0	81.5
Dalton plan or modification:									
Number	6	11	14	22	28	121	65	48	61
Per cent	1.4	2.3	3.4	4.6	6.8	25.4	15.9	11.6	12.8
Socialized class room procedure:									
Number	45	41	96	136	89	104	11	230	298
Per cent	11.0	8.6	23.5	28.6	21.8	21.8	2.7	56.3	62.7
Laboratory work in science: [3]									
Number	207		61		14		13	282	
Per cent	50.8		14.9		3.4		3.1	69.1	
Phonograph: [3]									
Number	18		31		75		48	124	
Per cent	4.4		7.6		18.4		11.7	30.4	
Other:									
Number	7		8		10		1	25	
Per cent	1.7		1.9		2.4		.2	6.0	

[1] Data on white schools from Monograph No. 6.
[2] This column applies to colored schools only.
[3] Data not available for white schools.

[97]

It will be remembered that in Chapter II certain general facts were given regarding the number of volumes and the current expenditures for the library in the schools of five States. The present section will furnish details on volumes per school and per pupil for the 688 schools of the Statistical group. Figure 16 displays the data for the different types of schools for Negroes only, and for the different sizes of schools for both colored and white children. The colored junior-senior high schools have a greater number of volumes per

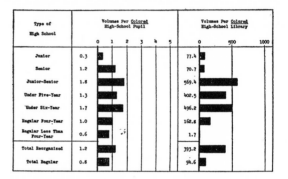

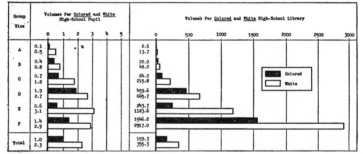

FIGURE 16.—Number of volumes in libraries of Negro high schools by type of school, and number of volumes in libraries of colored and white high schools by size of school

school and per pupil than the other schools. Also, it will be seen that when all reorganized schools are compared with regular schools, the former surpass the latter. In volumes per school the numbers are: Reorganized, 393.2; regular, 94.6. In volumes per pupil the numbers are: Reorganized, 1.2; regular, 0.8.

It will be observed in Figure 16 that in general the number of volumes per school and per pupil is greater in the larger

[98]

schools than in the smaller ones for both races; and in every
case the white schools far exceed the schools for Negroes.
For all schools combined, the volumes per white school are
355.3; for colored schools, 159.3. In volumes per pupil the
white schools have 2.3, while colored schools have only 1, an
advantage of more than 2 to 1 for the whites in both instances.

School librarian.—The manner in which the libraries of
357 Negro high schools are administered is reported in Table
44. It will be observed that the majority of the schools have
no special librarian, the library service being rendered by
members of the staff and student body devoting part time to
these duties.

TABLE 44.—*Numbers and percentages of Negro schools conducting their
libraries in the manners specified*

Method	Number	Per cent [1]	Method	Number	Per cent [1]
No librarian	37	8.7	Part-time librarian aided by staff members	35	8.3
Student librarian	52	12.3	Part-time librarian aided by students and staff members	22	5.2
Full-time librarian	44	10.4	No librarian; several members of staff and student body devote part time	73	17.3
Part-time librarian with no assistance	52	12.3			
Part-time librarian aided by students	42	9.9			

[1] 64, or 15.4 per cent, of the schools did not report.

9. SUPERVISION

Supervisory officers.—It is well known that supervision is
one of the weakest elements in the entire Negro educational
situation. It was revealed in Chapter VII that the principal
of the colored high school devoted only a small amount of
time to supervisory duties. In addition to the principal,
however, there are other officers having supervisory functions
in connection with Negro high schools.

The officers who visited the 393 schools replying to this
inquiry with frequencies of visits are listed in Table 45.
State officers made 134 visits to schools during 1929–30.
The average number of visits ranged from 2 to 5. No State
officers made more than 5 visits to any one school. The
county officers made more frequent visits to schools. The
highest average number of visits made to a given school by
any one county officer was 9. The average number of
visits made per school by county officials, excluding the miscellaneous group, ranged from 5 to 9. Miscellaneous county

officers combined made a total of 214 visits to 11 schools, making an average of 19 per school. Schools receiving visits from State and county officers are largely rural and village schools.

In considering the schools receiving visits from city supervisory officers, it was found that only in two instances was the average number of visits received per school less than 12. The officers and the average number of visits per school in these instances were the supervisor of foreign language, 8, and the supervisor of commercial subjects, 11. If the miscellaneous group of officers is eliminated the range in average number of visits per school made by city supervisory officers is found to be from 8 to 25. When this range in average number of visits is compared with the ranges of average number of visits made by State and county officers, it is seen that the rural schools, which need supervision most, receive the least.

TABLE 45.—*Supervisors visiting Negro high schools and frequency, of their visits*

Supervisory officers	Number of schools visited	Total visits	Supervisory officers	Number of schools visited	Total visits
State officers:			City officers—Continued.		
State supervisor	24	45	Supervisor of art	16	220
Director of Negro education	14	27	Supervisor of commercial subjects	5	56
State agents	9	20	Supervisor of English	14	169
State directors	6	10	Supervisor of foreign languages	6	49
State inspector	1	1	Supervisor of history and civics	11	152
Miscellaneous	6	31	Supervisor of home economics	25	614
Total		134	Supervisor of mathematics	14	350
County officers:			Supervisor of music	23	723
County superintendent	36	175	Supervisor of physical education	15	186
Jeanes supervisor	6	37	Supervisor of science	9	193
Agricultural agent	4	36	Supervisor of trades and vocations	24	595
Home demonstration agent	1	1	Miscellaneous	11	423
Miscellaneous	11	214	Total		4,985
Total		463			
City officers:			Miscellaneous officers	16	43
City superintendent	38	503			
Supervisor of secondary education	15	242	Grand total		5,625
General supervisor	33	510			

Supervisory functions.—In order to ascertain the type of service schools may expect of their supervisors, principals were asked to indicate what they considered the most important supervisory functions performed by supervisors. Table 46 shows the replies according to size of school. Three hundred and seventy, or 90.9 per cent, of the Survey scnools reported on this item.

Incentives for advancement.—What incentives are used to induce teachers to improve themselves? In order to secure information on this point data were obtained on the number of schools using certain methods. The incentives used and the percentages of schools using them are as follows: Advancement of certificate, 44.4; increase in salary, 35.6; promotion, 21.6; bonus, 6.1; other, 10.8. This investigation suggests the need of further study of the question of in-service training of teachers in Negro high schools.

TABLE 46.—*Numbers and percentages of Negro junior and senior high school principals indicating what they considered to be the most important supervisory functions performed by supervisors in their schools*

Functions	I		II		III		IV		V		VI		Total	
	Number	Per cent	Number	Per cent	Number	Per cent	Number	Per cent	Number	Per cent	Number	Per cent	Number	Per cent
1	2	3	4	5	6	7	8	9	10	11	12	13	14	15
Selecting and organizing materials	56	44.4	35	40.7	46	45.5	26	60.4	11	64.7	22	64.7	196	48.1
Demonstration teaching	24	19.0	16	18.6	25	24.7	11	25.5	4	23.5	4	11.7	84	20.6
Planning observation	18	14.2	8	9.3	20	19.8	7	16.2	3	17.6	8	23.5	64	15.7
Classroom visitation	71	56.3	67	77.9	67	66.3	31	72.0	16	94.1	33	97.0	285	70.0
Individual conferences	66	52.3	66	76.7	68	67.3	31	72.0	15	88.2	30	88.2	276	67.8
Group conferences	80	63.4	71	82.5	77	76.2	31	72.0	15	88.2	29	85.2	303	74.4
Stimulating use of teaching aids	47	37.3	49	56.9	54	53.4	17	39.5	11	64.7	20	58.8	198	48.6
Influencing professional growth	78	61.9	63	73.2	72	71.2	34	79.0	16	94.1	27	79.4	290	71.2
Encouraging self-rating	21	16.6	26	30.2	31	30.6	13	30.2	5	29.4	8	23.5	104	25.5
Measuring teaching efficiency	32	25.3	25	29.0	25	24.7	10	23.2	9	52.9	14	41.1	115	28.2
Measuring pupil achievement	41	32.5	37	43.0	43	42.5	22	51.1	9	52.9	21	61.7	173	42.5
Diagnostic testing and remedial teaching	24	19.0	24	27.9	26	25.7	15	34.8	6	35.2	16	47.0	111	27.2
Other	2	1.5	3	3.4	2	1.9	----	----	1	5.8	----	----	8	1.9
Total schools reporting	111	88.0	81	94.1	89	88.1	40	93.0	16	94.1	33	97.0	370	90.9

10. SUMMARY

From the preceding discussion it is seen that Negro secondary schools are employing in some degree most of the administrative and supervisory procedures in use by modern schools. In practically every case, however, the larger and the reorganized schools surpass the smaller and regular schools in the extent to which the methods and procedures are employed. Also, the schools for Negroes lag far behind those for whites in the use of these administrative and supervisory techniques.

1. THE BUILDING

The structures.—In general it may safely be said that one of the greatest contrasts between the colored and white races for educational expenditures has to do with capital outlay as represented by buildings and equipment. While exact statistics are not available, it is probable that this is as true of secondary education as of any other. Whatever expenditures have been made for secondary education for Negroes must of necessity be of recent date, since, as pointed out in Chapter V, most of the Negro high schools have been organized since the World War.

A comparison of the replies on date of organization and on date of construction shows that 67.8 per cent of the high schools were organized since 1915 and 65.9 per cent of the buildings have been constructed since that date. Table 47 shows the percentages of schools which are constructed of certain types of material. Of the 407 schools 31.6 per cent were frame, the percentage decreasing greatly with increase in the size of school. On the other hand, 50.1 per cent of the schools are of brick construction, the larger schools having a higher percentage than the smaller ones. Relatively fewer of the regular schools than of the reorganized are constructed of frame, and more of brick. Seventeen, or 4.2 per cent, of the schools made no reply concerning material of construction.

TABLE 47.—*Numbers and percentages of Negro high schools whose buildings are constructed of materials indicated, by size and type*

Materials of construction	Size groups						Types		Total [1]
	I	II	III	IV	V	VI	Regular	Reorganized	
1	2	3	4	5	6	7	8	9	10
Frame:									
Number	66	30	25	5	2	1	91	38	129
Per cent	52.3	34.8	24.7	11.6	11.7	2.9	30.1	36.1	31.6
Brick:									
Number	42	44	57	28	11	22	165	39	204
Per cent	33.3	62.7	56.4	65.1	64.7	62.8	54.6	37.1	50.1
Stone:									
Number	1	2		4	1	2	6	4	10
Per cent	.7	2.3		9.3	5.8	5.8	1.9	3.8	2.4
Concrete or stucco:									
Number	4	2	5	1	2	5	12	7	19
Per cent	3.1	2.3	4.9	2.3	11.7	14.7	3.9	6.6	4.6
Other:									
Number	10	3	5	5	1	4	19	9	28
Per cent	7.9	3.4	4.9	11.6	5.8	11.7	6.2	8.5	6.8

[1] 17 schools did not report.

State of repair.—Although the following data are derived from a question relying on subjective opinion for its answer, some indication at least is given of what the principals think about the condition of their school property. According to replies of the principals, Negro high-school buildings are in a good state of repair. In order to obtain information on this point principals were asked to indicate whether certain parts of their buildings were in a good, fair, or poor state of repair. Table 48 gives the replies to this inquiry.

TABLE 48.—*Numbers and percentages of Negro high-school principals reporting their buildings in various states of repair*

Features	Good		Fair		Poor	
	Number	Per cent	Number	Per cent	Number	Per cent
1	2	3	4	5	6	7
Outside paint	183	44.9	88	21.6	50	12.2
Inside paint	212	52.0	99	24.3	55	13.5
Windows	272	66.8	72	17.6	37	9.0
Woodwork	255	62.6	85	20.8	25	6.1
Steps	256	62.9	83	20.3	31	7.6
Masonry	259	63.6	55	13.5	18	4.4

2. SERVICE FACILITIES

Information concerning the service facilities of high schools for Negroes is supplied in Table 49. It will be noted that 49 per cent of the schools are heated by stoves, while 40 per cent have furnaces. Seventy-nine per cent have electricity. A feature of special importance concerning the next group of items in the table is the fact that 30 per cent of the schools have no fire protection facilities. This is particularly significant when viewed in the light of the previous statement that 49 per cent of the schools are heated by stoves. It is encouraging to note that only 2 per cent of the schools use a common drinking cup, and that 88 per cent have indoor or outdoor fountains. The importance of cleanliness seems not to be fully appreciated by the school authorities in a large number of communities, since only 62 per cent have provision for washing the hands. Another feature which has very important relations to health is the number of schools having ordinary outdoor surface toilets, 39 per cent reporting this kind of toilet facility. Still another factor having great bearing on cleanliness and health is janitorial service. According to evidence received, a large percentage of the Negro high schools had no regularly paid janitors.

TABLE 49.—*Numbers and percentages of Negro high schools having certain types of service facilities, by size of school*

Facilities	Size groups												Total	
	I		II		III		IV		V		VI			
	Number	Per cent	Number	Per cent	Number	Per cent	Number	Per cent	Number	Per cent	Number	Per cent	Number	Per cent
	2	3	4	5	6	7	8	9	10	11	12	13	14	15
Heating system:														
Stoves (wood or coal)	94	74.6	50	58.1	42	41.5	7	16.2	4	23.5	3	8.8	200	49.0
Grates (wood or coal)	4	3.1	1	1.1	1	0.9	1	2.3	---	---	---	---	9	1.0
Gas grates or heaters	16	12.6	8	9.3	4	3.9	7	16.2	---	---	4	11.7	39	9.0
Furnace	26	20.6	28	32.5	48	47.5	33	76.7	---	---	29	85.2	164	40.0
Other	---	---	1	1.1	2	1.9	1	2.3	1	5.8	1	2.9	5	1.0
Lighting system:														
None	12	9.5	3	3.4	1	.9	3	6.9	1	5.8	---	---	21	4.1
Lamps	9	7.1	7	8.1	2	1.9	---	---	---	---	---	---	14	5.1
Gaslight	6	4.7	4	4.6	4	3.9	---	---	---	---	---	---	14	3.4
Electricity	94	74.6	72	83.7	68	67.3	40	93.0	15	88.2	33	97.0	322	79.1
Other	---	---	1	1.1	1	.9	1	2.3	---	---	---	---	3	7.3
Fire protection facilities:														
None	62	49.2	31	36.0	22	21.7	5	11.6	3	17.6	23	67.6	123	30.2
Chemical fire extinguisher	32	25.3	26	30.2	48	47.5	9	20.9	10	58.8	---	---	148	36.3
Standpipe	3	2.3	4	4.6	8	7.9	4	9.3	---	---	2	8.8	22	5.4
Tubular slide	---	---	---	---	2	1.9	2	4.6	1	5.8	9	5.8	8	1.9
Stair wells	1	.7	1	1.1	8	7.9	1	2.3	3	17.6	9	26.4	28	6.8
Iron steps outside	6	4.7	14	16.2	16	15.8	11	25.5	4	23.5	11	32.3	61	14.9
Building fireproof construction	5	3.9	13	15.1	13	12.8	10	23.2	4	23.5	15	44.1	62	15.2
Drinking water supply and facilities:														
Shallow well	6	4.7	6	6.9	3	2.9	2	4.6	1	5.8	1	---	15	3.6
Deep well	1	16.6	18	20.9	12	11.9	---	---	---	---	---	---	54	13.2
Common cup	5	3.9	1	1.1	3	2.9	---	---	---	---	---	---	9	2.2
Individual cups	29	23.0	13	15.1	14	13.8	3	6.9	1	5.8	1	2.9	61	14.9
Outdoor fountains	31	24.6	26	30.2	37	36.6	14	32.5	9	52.9	10	29.4	127	31.2
Indoor fountains	55	43.6	40	46.5	60	59.4	38	88.3	12	70.5	33	97.0	233	57.2

[105]

TABLE 49.—*Numbers and percentages of Negro high schools having certain types of service facilities, by size of school—Contd.*

Facilities	Size groups												Total	
	I		II		III		IV		V		VI			
	Number	Per cent	Number	Per cent	Number	Per cent	Number	Per cent	Number	Per cent	Number	Per cent	Number	Per cent
1	2	3	4	5	6	7	8	9	10	11	12	13	14	15
Washing and bathing facilities:														
Hand basins	67	53.1	52	60.4	65	64.3	30	69.7	11	64.7	30	88.2	255	62.6
Toilet facilities:														
Outdoor	76	60.3	42	48.8	31	30.6	7	16.2	3	17.6	1	2.9	160	39.3
Outdoor flush	14	11.1	9	10.4	10	9.9	5	11.6	3	17.6			41	10.0
Indoor chemical	2	1.6	2	2.3	1	.9					1	2.9	6	1.4
Indoor flush	30	23.8	33	38.3	56	55.4	31	72.0	11	64.7	15	44.1	176	43.2
Other facilities	195		184		228		131		58		149			

[106]

3. ROOMS

Instructional rooms.—Facts regarding number and kind of special rooms to which Negro secondary-school pupils have access are presented in Table 50. For almost all classes of rooms there is a decided rise in the percentage of schools having them as the size of school increases. A significant difference here between regular and reorganized schools favors the latter, except in the case of industrial arts rooms.

Special rooms for instructional purposes are important, but of equal importance is the special instructional equipment for these rooms. While a few high schools for Negroes have adequate, modern equipment and facilities for instruction in specialized courses, such as the sciences, and arts, general observation reveals a considerable deficiency in this regard. Negro high schools were found in several communities to be using equipment which had been discarded by the white high schools.

Service rooms.—As will be observed from Table 51, the larger high schools have a distinct advantage over the smaller schools in the percentage having additional service rooms and facilities.

TABLE 50.—*Numbers and percentages of Negro high schools having various kinds of special rooms for instructional purposes, by size and type*

Rooms	Size groups						Types		Total
	I	II	III	IV	V	VI	Regular	Reorganized	
1	2	3	4	5	6	7	8	9	10
Chemistry:									
Number	6	16	25	20	10	21	63	35	98
Per cent	4.7	18.6	24.7	46.5	58.8	61.7	20.8	33.3	24.0
Physics:									
Number	2	11	20	10	5	16	34	30	64
Per cent	1.5	12.7	19.8	23.2	29.4	47.0	11.2	28.5	15.7
Biology:									
Number	7	17	28	13	6	16	56	31	87
Per cent	5.5	19.7	27.7	30.2	35.2	47.0	18.5	29.5	21.3
General science:									
Number	15	21	21	8	6	14	53	32	85
Per cent	11.9	24.4	20.7	18.6	35.2	41.1	17.5	30.4	20.8
Household arts:									
Number	46	48	62	34	12	32	169	65	234
Per cent	36.5	55.8	61.3	79.0	70.5	94.1	55.9	61.9	57.4
Industrial arts:									
Number	29	26	41	23	8	28	116	39	155
Per cent	23.0	30.2	40.5	53.4	47.0	82.3	38.4	37.1	38.

TABLE 50.—*Numbers and percentages of Negro high schools having various kinds of special rooms for instructional purposes, by size and type—* Continued

Rooms	Size groups						Types		Total
	I	II	III	IV	V	VI	Regular	Reorganized	
1	2	3	4	5	6	7	8	9	10
Drawing and art:									
Number	2	4	12	4	4	21	26	21	47
Per cent	1.5	4.6	11.8	9.3	23.5	61.7	8.6	20.0	11.5
Music:									
Number	12	17	22	15	6	20	59	33	92
Per cent	9.5	19.7	21.7	34.8	35.2	58.8	19.5	31.4	22.6
Commercial art:									
Number		1	8	10	2	11	19	13	32
Per cent		1.1	7.9	23.2	11.7	32.3	6.2	12.3	7.8
Agriculture:									
Number									
Per cent									
Others:									
Number	19	23	33	15		8	84	14	98
Per cent	15.0	26.7	32.6	34.8		23.5	27.8	13.3	24.0
Total schools reporting special rooms:									
Number	75	72	84	40	14	33	235	83	318
Per cent of schools in group	59.5	83.7	83.1	93.0	82.3	97.0	77.8	79.0	78.1

TABLE 51.—*Numbers and percentages of Negro high schools having additional service rooms and facilities by size of school*

Rooms and facilities	Size group												Total	
	I		II		III		IV		V		VI			
	Number	Per cent	Number	Per cent	Number	Per cent	Number	Per cent	Number	Per cent	Number	Per cent	Number	Per cent
1	2	3	4	5	6	7	8	9	10	11	12	13	14	15
Teacher's offices	38	26.1	36	41.8	26	25.7	12	27.9	6	35.2	6	17.6	119	29.2
Teachers' rest room	7	5.5	18	20.9	17	16.8	11	25.5	8	47.0	20	58.8	81	19.9
Students' rest room	5	3.9	8	9.3	15	14.8	9	20.9	3	17.6	8	23.5	48	11.7
Dental clinic			2	2.3	3	2.9	3	6.9	3	17.6	2	5.8	13	3.1
General clinic	1	.7	2	2.3	5	4.9	6	13.9			11	32.3	25	6.1
Students' activity room	11	8.7	10	11.6	9	8.9	4	9.3	3	17.6	4	11.7	41	10.0
Custodian's room	9	7.1	15	17.4	18	17.8	15	34.8	2	11.7	16	47.0	75	18.4
Gymnasium	1	.7	6	6.9	11	10.8	9	16.2	5	29.4	12	35.2	42	10.3
Auditorium	81	64.2	72	83.7	81	80.1	30	69.7	15	88.2	27	79.4	306	75.1
Gymnasium-auditorium	20	15.8	18	20.9	25	24.7	17	39.5	3	17.6	15	44.1	98	24.0
Study hall	4	3.1	10	11.6	12	11.8	7	16.2	3	17.6	10	29.4	46	11.3
Auditorium study hall	37	29.3	29	33.7	33	32.6	18	41.8	8	47.0	16	47.0	141	34.6
Auditorium-clinic room	55	43.6	34	39.5	45	44.5	19	44.1	6	35.2	8	23.5	167	41.0
Swimming pool					3	2.9			1	5.8	2	5.8	6	1.4
Cafeteria	9	7.1	10	11.6	14	13.8	15	34.8	7	41.1	28	82.3	83	20.3
Curtains for stage	60	47.6	54	62.7	55	54.4	27	62.7	14	82.3	24	70.5	234	57.4
Scenery for stage	21	16.6	20	23.2	34	33.6	10	23.2	8	47.0	15	44.1	108	26.5
Motion-picture machine	4	3.1	11	12.7	14	13.8	11	25.5	4	23.5	15	44.1	59	14.4
Stereopticon machine	3	2.3	7	8.1	8	7.9	5	11.6	7	41.1	11	32.3	41	10.0

4. *IMPROVEMENTS AND ADDITIONS*

Of the 407 schools represented in the study, 56 indicated that they had added one or more new buildings during the past five years. Of these, 41 are regular and 15 are reorganized schools. Of the 91 schools adding rooms, 73 are regular and 18 are reorganized. Ten schools made enlargements of their plants, and 19 improved the landscape. Other miscellaneous improvements were made by 49 schools.

5. *SUMMARY*

Most of the buildings housing Negro high schools have been constructed comparatively recently, and, according to the opinion of the principal, are in a good state of repair. Many schools do not have janitors; only a few have wash basins. The general service conveniences, such as toilet, heating, and fire protection facilities are meager and often of unsatisfactory types. Additional instructional rooms are found in a high percentage of the larger and the reorganized schools, which, in general, surpass the smaller and the regular schools in this respect.

CHAPTER X : SUMMARY, CONCLUSIONS, AND RECOMMENDATIONS

1. IMPORTANCE OF THE EVIDENCE

"The ultimate value of the school system of a State is the character and extent of the educational opportunities it offers its children." [1]

The articles of the constitutions of the various States relating to education make no distinction among their children, the assumption being in every case that all the children shall be given an equal educational opportunity. That this ideal is not attained in many States is a fact which is increasingly becoming the concern of educators and statesmen throughout the land. Among the groups affected by an unequal distribution of educational facilities in the States having separate schools, the Negro is by far the greatest sufferer. This disadvantage is pronounced at all levels of education, and, of course, is accentuated at the secondary level.

Almost everyone at all conversant with the matter has recognized the need for improvement, and, while certain facts were known regarding the deficiencies, no body of objective knowledge of sufficient scope was available concerning recent developments and present status to be used as an authoritative guide in formulating principles and policies and in evolving practices in secondary education for Negroes. The present study is an attempt to supply this need. It does not purport to cover the entire field, but rather to reveal some of the major facts and tendencies and to suggest the value of other lines of investigation which should be followed.

The report of the study has presented certain facts relating to the following: A brief sketch of the educational background of the Negro and his present social, economic, and religious life; the availability of secondary educational

[1] Texas Educational Survey Commission. Texas Educational Survey Report, Vol. VIII, General Report. Austin, Tex., 1925, p. 39.

facilities for Negroes in States maintaining separate schools; '
and the present status of Negro high schools with respect to
organization, curriculum, and extracurriculum offerings,
pupils, staff, administration and supervision, and housing
and equipment. This chapter concerns itself with a summary
of the findings and the presentation of certain conclusions
and recommendations.

2. FINDINGS CONCERNING AVAILABILITY OF SECONDARY-SCHOOL FACILITIES

1. The 9,420,747 Negroes in the 16 States studied comprise
23.1 per cent of the total population of these States. Sixty-
seven per cent live in rural areas; and 15.1 per cent are
illiterate in comparison with 2.6 per cent of illiterates for
whites in the same States.

2. Of the 1,067,921 Negroes of high-school age in 16
Southern States, only 101,998 (or 9.5 per cent) are enrolled
in public high schools, as contrasted with 33.5 per cent of the
white population of high-school age in the same States.

3. The ratio of Negro public high-school pupils to Negro
population is 11 per 1,000, corresponding to 34 white public
high-school pupils per 1,000 white population.

4. The percentage of white pupils enrolled in high school
is more than three times as great as the corresponding
percentage for colored pupils, being 14.2 and 4.5, respectively.

5. The variation among the States in the percentage each
high-school grade enrollment is of the total high-school
enrollment is quite marked in Negro schools; for whites
the corresponding percentages are nearly constant.

6. The ratio of number of teachers to Negro population of
high-school age in 16 Southern States is 1 to 211; for whites
it is 1 to 60 in these same States. To equalize these ratios
would require a total of 17,798 Negro teachers, or 12,758
more than are employed at present.

7. The costs per pupil for white and colored high-school
teachers' salaries are, respectively, $34.18 and $22.65 in
10 Southern States affording comparable data. To bring
the cost per Negro pupil up to the whites would require an
additional expenditure of $1,175,182, or 51 per cent more than
is at present being spent.

8. The cost per person of high-school age for white and colored high-school teachers' salaries is, respectively, $11.47 and $2.16. To make the two races equal in this regard in the 16 Southern States studied, and on the basis of figures for 1930, would require an additional annual expenditure for Negroes of $9,937,944, or 430 per cent, more than is at present being spent.

9. Of 1,140 Negro high schools reported by 15 States, only 506 offer 4 years of work.

10. Only 39 per cent of the 4-year high schools are available to Negroes living in rural areas; these constitute 67.4 per cent of the total Negro population.

11. The public schools which are accredited number 244, which includes only 60 per cent of all the Negro schools reporting.

12. Of the 1,413 counties in the 15 States, 230, having a Negro population constituting 12.5 per cent of more or the total population, had no high-school facilities for Negroes at all. The Negro population in these counties is 1,397,304, 158,939 of whom are of high-school age.

13. Of the remaining counties, 195, in which Negroes constitute 12.5 per cent or more of the population, had no 4-year high schools for colored children. The Negro population in these counties is 1,671,501, of whom 197,242 are of high-school age.

14. In five States the amount spent for the transportation of Negro high-school pupils is $30,000, as compared with $5,000,000 for white high-school pupils in the same States. This means that $166 are spent for the transportation of white high-school pupils for every $1 spent for the transportation of Negro high-school pupils, while the ratio of white and Negro children of high-school age in the same States is only 2 to 1.

5. FINDINGS CONCERNING ORGANIZATION

1. Although three-fourths of the schools reporting are regular, they enroll only three-fifths of the pupils; while the reorganized schools, constituting only a fourth of the total, enroll two-fifths of the pupils.

2. Nearly a third (30 per cent) of the schools are far removed from the homes of their pupils. The area which each of these schools serves is approximately 30 square miles.

3. Nearly half the schools have three teachers or fewer.

4. Two-thirds of the schools have been started since the beginning of the World War.

5. Eighty-six per cent of the accredited schools have been accredited since 1920.

6. The past 15 years have been the period of greatest growth in secondary education for Negroes.

4. FINDINGS CONCERNING THE CURRICULUM AND EXTRACURRICULUM

1. Large schools offer more electives and require fewer subjects and courses than the smaller schools.

2. Reorganized schools have more academic and fewer vocational curriculums than regular schools.

3. English holds first place as a required and last as an elective subject.

4. Foreign language ranks first as an elective and fifth as a required subject.

5. The percentages of schools requiring mathematics and science tend to decrease and those offering elective work in these subjects to increase in the upper high-school grades.

6. A small percentage of the schools offer work in commercial subjects, music, and fine arts.

7. The smaller schools have dropped more courses than they have added during the past five years, while the reverse has been true for the larger schools.

8. Foreign language is the only subject in which more courses have been dropped than added Of the 69 courses in foreign language dropped, 54 are Latin.

9. Of the 209 courses added by the 291 schools during the past five years, 90 were in science, 83 in social science, 59 in household and industrial arts, 49 in foreign language. Other additions were: Commerce, 35; mathematics, 30; agriculture, 21; education and related subjects, 16; English, 14; music, 12; health and physical education, 12; fine arts, 1.

10. Of the 119 courses dropped, 69 were in foreign language. Other eliminations were: Household and industrial

arts, 36; science, 28; social studies, 16; mathematics, 14; commerce, 10; education and related subjects, 8; health and physical education, 7; agriculture, 6.

11. Eighteen schools added courses in Negro history during the past five years.

12. The larger schools offer more extracurriculum activities than do the smaller schools.

13. In general the white schools are superior to the colored schools in richness of curriculum and extracurriculum offerings.

6. FINDINGS CONCERNING PUPILS

1. High-school enrollment of Negro pupils has increased steadily since 1892. During the past decade it has been exceedingly marked. During this period the percentage of increase of colored pupils has exceeded that for whites.

2. The enrollment of Negro girls in high school is greater than that of boys. This disproportion increases in the higher grades. The rate of increase of enrollment of girls in recent years is also greater than that of boys.

3. The disproportion between high-school enrollment of Negro boys and girls is less in reorganized than in regular schools.

4. Registration of Negro pupils in academic curriculums is greater in reorganized than in regular schools, and tends to increase as the size of school increases. For general curriculums the converse is true for both type and size.

5. A larger percentage of the enrollment is graduated from smaller schools than from the larger schools.

6. A larger percentage of the enrollment is graduated from the regular than from the reorganized schools.

7. A larger percentage of Negro boys than girls continue their education after high-school graduation.

8. A larger percentage of white than Negro pupils enroll in the commercial curriculum.

9. Although a larger percentage of Negro than white high-school graduates continue their education, the whites surpass the Negroes in the percentage of their total high-school enrollment graduated from high school.

6. FINDINGS CONCERNING TEACHERS

1. The typical Negro high-school teacher gives instruction in two or more subject fields.

2. A number of unusual teaching combinations is found among Negro high-school teachers.

3. The pupil-teacher ratio is much higher for colored teachers than for white teachers in all sizes and types of schools.

4. The typical Negro high-school teacher has three and one-third years of college training. Two-thirds of the teachers have bachelors' or masters' degrees.

5. Nearly three-fourths of the Negro high-school teachers received their academic training in private colleges.

6. Teachers in rural sections have much less training than those in urban centers. The median number of years of college training for those in the open country is 2.8 as compared with 4.5 for those in large cities. Teachers in rural sections also receive less salary.

7. The average colored high-school teacher has 26.8 semester hours of training in the field of education, and 6.3 semester hours in practice teaching.

8. The average length of experience of Negro secondary teachers is 7 years. Fifty-seven per cent have had more than 5 years of experience.

9. The less training a Negro high-school teacher possesses, the smaller his salary.

10. The median annual salary of colored high-school teachers in the Southern States is $956; for white teachers throughout the country it is $1,479 in unselected and $1,601 in selected small high schools.

7. FINDINGS CONCERNING PRINCIPALS

1. The typical Negro high-school principal is a married man, 42 years of age.

2. He has had 4.6 years of college training, has completed 31.5 semester hours in the field of education, and has attended summer school during the past 5 years.

3. He has had 17.3 years of educational experience and has been in his present position 5.9 years, while the average tenure of white principals of small high schools is less than 3 years.

[115]

4. The average Negro high-school principal teaches 18 hours a week and devotes only 7 hours to supervision. The smaller the school the greater is the amount of time the principal devotes to teaching.

5. The Negro principal's salary is only $1,325 a year as compared with $2,454 for white principals of small high schools for the country as a whole. Negro principals receiving annual salaries of $1,500 or less constitute 61.2 per cent of the total, while the corresponding percentage for white principals of the small high school for the country as a whole is 7.6.

8. FINDINGS CONCERNING ADMINISTRATION AND SUPERVISION

1. Eighty-four per cent of the Negro high schools share their buildings with other school units, as compared with 48 per cent of the white schools in the country at large.

2. Fewer schools of the larger size groups than of the smaller ones share their buildings.

3. Of 196 schools replying, 47 per cent have enrollments in excess of their capacity. These surpluses are handled in 14 per cent of the cases by shortened periods and in 26 per cent by temporary classrooms.

4. Fewer reorganized schools than regular schools promote by grades.

5. A larger percentage of the reorganized schools and of the large schools than of the regular and small schools give and use the results of psychological and standardized tests. In both these regards the white schools greatly surpass the colored schools.

6. The large and reorganized schools make more provision for individual differences than do the small and regular schools.

7. The large and reorganized schools surpass the small and regular schools in extended services, such as summer school, part-time or continuation classes, opportunity classes, etc.

8. Larger schools have better provision than smaller schools for care and promotion of health.

9. A large percentage of the Negro schools is making use of modern procedures and techniques of instruction, although they are still behind white schools in this regard.

9. FINDINGS CONCERNING HOUSING AND EQUIPMENT

1. Negro high-school buildings were generally reported to be in a good state of repair.

2. A large percentage of Negro high schools is without janitors.

3. Few wash basins are found in Negro high schools.

4. In general the percentage of schools having science laboratories and other special instructional rooms is small. As is to be expected the larger and the reorganized schools have an advantage over the smaller and regular schools in this regard.

5. Fifty-six of the Negro high schools had added new buildings to their plants during the past 5 years; 91 had added new rooms; 10 schools enlarged their plants, and 19 improved the landscape; 49 made other miscellaneous improvements.

6. Modern lighting and drinking-water facilities seem to be possessed by a large percentage of the Negro schools.

7. Furnace heating and modern fire protection, hand-washing and sanitary toilet facilities were lacking in a large percentage of the schools.

8. As a rule the Negro high school is greatly inferior with respect to housing and equipment to the white high school in the same community. Frequently the colored school uses discarded materials and equipment from the white school.

10. CONCLUSIONS

From the evidence assembled and analyzed for this report the following inferences may be drawn:

1. The Negro has shown remarkable avidity in accepting the secondary-school facilities available to him.

2. A close relationship is apparent between availability and popularization of secondary education among Negroes.

3. Although the trend of the Negro population is from rural to urban centers, the fact that two-thirds still live in the rural centers suggests the need for a larger share of the secondary-school facilities in these localities.

4. Since, as demonstrated in the National Survey of the Education of Teachers most of the Negro elementary teachers

receive all their training in secondary schools, the improvement and extension of elementary education among Negroes and the reduction of the high percentage of illiteracy depends on the improvement and extension of secondary-school facilities.

5. The accessibility of Negro high schools to the pupils they serve is a problem of serious proportions.

6. The large school is far superior to the small school in offering the advantages of secondary education.

7. The reorganized school is in general superior to the regular school in offering secondary-school facilities.

8. The small Negro high school seems to be making an effort to simplify its program of studies.

9. Although foreign language holds first place as an elective and fifth place as a required subject, it is gradually losing ground.

10. Despite the fact that there seems to be a growing interest among Negro schools in studying Negro history, the offering in this subject is extremely meager.

11. A definite tendency is observed in Negro high schools to change their programs of study to meet modern conditions.

12. Negro girls appear to be favored over boys in the proportion who are sent to high school.

13. The fact that larger percentages of Negro pupils enrolled in small and regular high schools than in large and reorganized schools are graduated is probably a result of the pupils' objectives rather than of superior offerings of the schools.

14. A direct relationship exists between the size of place, size of school, amount of training, and salaries of Negro high-school teachers.

15. The typical Negro high-school teacher has a fair degree of academic and professional training, but is greatly overburdened and underpaid.

16. The typical principal of the Negro high school is a teaching principal rather than a supervisory and administrative officer.

17. A large proportion of Negro high schools are inadequately provided with equipment and facilities to maintain and promote health.

18. In view of the lack of public-school facilities for Negroes and of the preponderance of Negro public-school teachers graduated from them the private colleges and universities still have a strong relationship and a responsibility to the education of the Negro.

19. The differences in secondary-school facilities between the white and colored races are in most factors noticeable and in practically every instance of major importance in favor of the whites. This is true whether the colored schools of the Southern States are compared with the white schools of the same States or with the white schools for the country at large.

20. The great progress made in secondary education for the colored race has been largely the result of an increasingly sympathetic attitude toward Negro education in the States maintaining separate schools.

21. In spite of the progress made in secondary education for Negroes, they have a long way to go before they reach the optimum point in the matter of high-school enrollment. Meanwhile, a great source of wealth and power is going to waste in the thousands of Negro youth of high-school age who are not in school because of the absence of facilities.

22. Because of the lack of educational facilities and the general inadequacy of secondary-school offerings, the Negro race is facing the competition of American life at an enormous disadvantage.

23. If the educational chasm existing between the two races is ever bridged or lessened, improvement in school conditions must go forward at a much more rapid rate than it has in the past. Negroes can not meet the exacting standards of modern civilization with intelligence, skill, and courage, and keep pace with the tempo of American life with an education which lags behind 10, 15, or 20 years.

24. That a growing number of persons in every section of the country is becoming conscious of the problems in Negro education is evidenced by many of the facts gathered during this study.

11. RECOMMENDATIONS

In view of the findings and conclusions herein presented, the following recommendations are made:

1. Principals and teachers of Negro high schools should more vigorously address themselves to modernizing those practices and procedures over which they have control.

2. Principals and teachers of Negro high schools should exhibit greater interest in cooperating in national studies and other movements designed to improve educational conditions among Negroes.

3. In the course of the investigation many studies have suggested themselves as fruitful fields for study which should be attacked by the staffs of Negro high schools, by graduate students, by State and city school administrative officers, and by other interested agencies. Among them are the following:

(a) A study of the accessibility of secondary-school facilities for Negroes in certain localities, counties, and States.

(b) Factors affecting the variation of support of secondary education for Negroes in the different counties and districts of certain States.

(c) Factors affecting the elimination and retardation of Negro secondary-school pupils.

(d) Influences and trends of curriculum changes in individual secondary schools.

(e) A vocational education survey for Negroes, including a study of vocational guidance and vocational opportunity.

(f) A Negro student personnel study at the high-school level.

(g) Availability of elementary education for Negroes in selected States and communities in relation to secondary and higher education.

(h) In the light of (e), (f), and (g), an intensive investigation of programs of studies and curriculums of Negro high schools.

4. In view of their manifest superiority in most respects, it is recommended that as rapidly as possible school authorities establish larger high schools for Negroes by consolidating smaller ones already existing and by merging school districts.

5. In line with recommendation 4 it is urged that increased transportation facilities be provided in order to make such consolidated schools accessible to the greatest number of children.

6. While recognizing the effectiveness in many communities of the regular type of high school, because of the apparent superiority of the reorganized type of school in many of the major educational criteria, it is recommended that, whenever a change is contemplated, or wherever a new school is to be established, the merits of the reorganized type of school be carefully considered.

7. In view of the importance to a people of a knowledge of their historical background, it is recommended that as rapidly as possible courses in Negro history be added to the programs of studies of Negro high schools.

8. It is urgently recommended that steps be taken as early as possible to provide secondary-school facilities for the 158,-939 Negroes of high-school age in the 230 counties of the South in which no Negro high schools exist; and 4-year facilities for the 197,242 Negroes of high-school age in the 195 counties where no 4-year high schools are in operation.

9. Finally, it is recommended that the support of secondary education be so increased and equitably distributed and the standards so raised as to approximate as nearly as possible an equal educational opportunity for all youth, regardless of condition and race.